nappturosity

How To Create Fabulous Natural Hair and Locs

by **erin**shell**anthony**

praisefornappturosity

"(You've) produced a book that is chock full of…guidance to keep your hair naturally beautiful!" - **Patrice Yursik, Creator of Afrobella.com**

"When I started locking my hair there were no books to educate us on the joys and challenges of going natural. When I read Nappturosity, I was overjoyed by the fact that it spoke directly to the concerns I had when I went natural. Nappturosity was not only fun to read but informative – I call it the Nappy Bible!" - **Yetta Young, Executive Producer of The Vagina Monologues**

"Erin Anthony has done an awesome job in conveying the importance of caring for natural hair! Nappturosity is informative, inspiring and absolutely necessary! A must read for women with natural hair and those considering taking the journey!"
- **Michelle Lewis, Producer & Director New Growth: A Natural Progression, Houston, TX**

"I was learning…through trial and error. When I found Nappturosity, I was AMAZED! Everything in this book answered all the questions I wanted to know! erin shell anthony, thank you so much for coming up with this…you have answered our call!" - **LaToya Rivers, Producer of the Natural Beauties of KC Natural Hair Show, Kansas City, MO**

"Out of all the…books I have read, this is one of the BEST! Very informative. Thank you for celebrating our God-given hair and keeping it natural." - **Johnnie Reid**

"I am so happy that I bought your book. I have been natural for almost 10 years. Once I started reading your book so many blanks were filled in for me. Reading it was and is like an "aha" moment." - **Lynette Simmons**

"Through my process, I purchased a lot of different books and went to a lot of different websites…and Nappturosity was the first to offer realistic and usable solutions! When I tried the suggestions in the book, I saw results!" -**Tonia Baker**

"You approached your audience with love of their God-given hair instead of just a hair style. That's the key element that is missing in so many natural hair books. I personally love my hair and no longer wish and dream that God had made my hair differently!" - **Arlanda Darkwa, Certified Sisterlocks Consultant and Trainer**

"While on the road to natural hair freedom, it was Erin who inspired me to reach my goal of locking...watching her transition and seeing her devote her life to wellness and "all things natural" has been.. well, infectious! You WILL want to catch this!" - **Safiya Bell**

"I just want to start by saying thank you for taking the time to research this information and for writing such a fabulous book. You have made my loc journey a breeze, as well as changed the lives of my friends and how they view their daughters hair. I love the entire book and have tried all of the recipes appropriate for loc wearers, as well as the natural commerical products that you have suggested (all receiving rave reviews)!" -**Brandy Watkins**

To all the women who will make the transition

to natural hair and to those who already have,

thank you for showing me your struggle,

your journey, and your successes,

so that I can pass these lessons on to help others.

Peace, Blessings and Beautiful Hair.

table of contents

Principle # 2: We Appreciate Our Texture

Principle # 3: We Know Our Ingredients

Principle #4: We Are Fabulous!

1

what is nappturosity?

Nappturosity is the art of developing remarkable, attention-grabbing natural hair…hair that is all your own and absolutely fabulous in its own reign and glory!

In the essence of your every curl is a regal nature that speaks, proclaiming truth, love and a beautiful being. Congratulations and welcome to the ultimate guide to the world of natural hair and loc care!

The purpose of this book is to explain the HOW of natural hair and loc care for afro-textured or curly hair, for people of African descent.

- You'll learn about the most up-to-date methods to naturally care for your hair.

- You'll understand the definitions of the ingredients on the label of a product, as well as what products and tools to use for fabulous results, and which ones to avoid!

- You'll enjoy gorgeous pictures that display both the classic and recent innovations in styling techniques.

- You'll also learn what no one else can teach you – how to produce the results you've always wanted with your own hair! We'll enhance your relationship with your hair while developing your own personal Natural Hair Manifesto that will help you to take a realistic look at what you have, assess where you want to be, and manifest your personal, attainable goals for your hair!

You probably fall into one of three groups: Transitioners, looking for information on the how-to of going natural; Newly Natural, where you've just gone natural and are still getting adjusted to your new texture; or Experienced, as you have been natural for a while and want to bring a new or more defined style, flavor and kick to your hair!

That's right - every little kink, every loose curl, all that beautiful new growth – you have it all for a reason, and together we're going to create a serious love/love relationship between you and your hair – or if you already have that, let's develop it to the point where you just can't stand YOURSELF! Sound good? Great!

The reason that I am a proponent of natural hair and want to provide extraordinary information regarding its care is because of the struggle that I had finding information and understanding my options. I grew up believing that my hair was not 'good' or 'worthwhile' and did everything in my power to disguise its natural beauty.

I wore every weave and chemical process imaginable, and still was not happy! Something was missing. The only compliments that I would receive would be when I wore hair that wasn't mine, either in the form of a weave or braids. I interacted with friends who were going through the same process, and no one knew any answers to our circumstance. Then, one day, IT happened. I knew I couldn't take dry, stringy, used-to-be-long-but-not-anymore hair, so I woke up around 2am one morning and cut ALL of my relaxer off, and promptly sat down on the floor with my head in my hands and cried.

Really – I was in shock. I didn't have a clue about how to style my hair, but at the same time, my cry was a relief, and a letting go of the years of bondage to someone else's idea of what was beautiful and fabulous. This experience began my trek around the country, from Los Angeles to

New York, to St. Louis, to Dallas and other cities to find the best styling options, the best products, and eventually, to open a natural hair salon that focused on delivering these finds in a welcoming atmosphere.   This refuge was for me and so many others, a cultural center, a place where we could come and release our frustrations, find understanding and learn how to properly rock our natural beauty!

I loved wearing my hair in various natural and braided styles, and after several years, transitioned to Sisterlocks™, and have provided guiding tools, advice and support to countless friends, clients and colleagues as they conducted their own personal transition to natural hair and locs over the years.

It was beautiful watching clients leave looking fabulous in their glorious nappturosity, but they would also communicate with me how working through my program left them educated, inspired and empowered, and soon, they began helping others do the same! When I saw how the information that I am now sharing in this book was changing lives, I decided that every Nappturous Diva or Nappturous Diva in-the-making deserves to know this information, and as we all learn, we elevate our collective understanding.

This information is what is now, hot, new and ready to be served up for the people! Any individual who has wanted to have the answer to their natural hair questions, from how to conduct a modern, personalized hair care regime to the top five mistakes cultivated lock wearers make, will find the "how and why" here.

Information on what hair is and why black women should culturally and spiritually consider natural hair abounds in books and on the internet. The intrigue, historical relevance and psychological effects of slavery on natural hair has been solidly established and gained respect in the black community, so, in giving homage to the pioneers who have documented this historical data, we will simply refer to their resources for that information, and it will not be covered in this book.

There are so many women who are interested in going natural, have natural hair, or have primary responsibility over someone with natural hair, **who just want to know how to cycle through the process of managing, developing, and styling natural hair!**

If that statement made you nod your head, this book is for YOU! But, before you throw on your Angela Davis 'fro or start cooking up products in your kitchen like Lisa Price of Carol's Daughter ingeniously did, allow me to introduce you to the principles of a Nappturous Diva so that YOU too can be formally inducted into our Nappturous Diva-hood!

The Nappturous Diva PRINCIPLES:

1. **RELATIONSHIP: We Develop a Relationship with Our Hair** – We have a plan for our hair, and we listen to what our hair needs and find solutions for challenges. Caring for our hair becomes a ritual and we use that time to assess what is working and what is not. We're flexible!

2. **APPRECIATION: We Appreciate Our Texture** – We know that every texture has its Celebrations as well as its Challenges. We are continually discovering and appreciating the uniqueness of our God-given curls and coils, and styling it in ways that complement our texture.

3. **KNOWLEDGE: We Know Our Ingredients!** – Our hair is, in part, our own creation. The extent that we feed our hair internally and externally with ingredients in the products we use shapes the health and condition of our hair. We use products that have ingredients that support the greatest good of our hair.

4. **CONFIDENCE: We are Fabulous** – Translated, we are confident! If we have it, we work it. We never let an ill-informed person dictate how we feel about our hair. We choose to feel great about how we wear every single strand!

A Nappturous Diva is an empowered woman who has embraced her own nappturosity, and when she looks in the mirror, loves the crowning glory she sees. She's been through a multitude of hair storms and experienced the ups and downs of the hair roller coaster.

She is solid in her beliefs and determined to share the knowledge with those who ask. Once a Nappturous Diva learns how to take care of her hair, she has the option to use the salon to meet her needs for pampering and out of the occasional necessity, and pockets the money and time saved! As Nappturous Divas, we're educated, inspired and informed!

10reasons
Why Natural Hair is Fabulous!

REASON #1: Nothing looks better on you than something that was designed FOR you! You wouldn't walk out of the house with jeans that gape at the waist or wear the almost perfect jacket you bought on clearance that was 2 sizes too big!

You would take the item to a seamstress to have it customized just for you! Your own natural hair was created just for you – it was designed to look fabulous on your head!

REASON #2: You experience a feeling that I call "hair emancipation"! This beautiful wave of relief combined with supreme confidence will first occur when you look at yourself for the first time with your first natural 'do.

If you're natural, you probably can identify with running your fingers through your natural hair for the first time, patting it in disbelief, pulling the curls to see the length, and just relishing an overall amazement.

8

Note: Hair emancipation may occur at the actual time the relaxer gets trimmed off the ends of your natural hair, or maybe a little later, but it does eventually come!

REASON #3: Your entire quality of life changes. Long gone will be the days that you couldn't roll the windows down and let the wind blow through your hair.

You won't have to think twice about going swimming or participating in regular fitness programs – you can exercise and take better care of your body because you aren't so concerned about your hair.

You'll also find yourself less worried about getting your hair wet from the rain (especially if you have locs), and you just may enjoy that umbrella-less dash to the car when it's starting to sprinkle!

REASON #4: Nappturous Divas enjoy compliments more! Although it's great to have someone compliment an extension, in the back of your mind, you know that what they are complimenting isn't really you.

We certainly may have rocked a weave at some point, and have nothing against sisters who do, but there is nothing like the feeling of wearing your nappturous hair, and walking down the street, through the offering line at church, or sitting down at a table in a restaurant, and noticing an approving smile and nod from a nearby observer.

Loc wearers term this look the 'loc'd glance', a simple look of acknowledgement from another loc wearer. It's a kindred family that shares a multitude of stories in a simple, knowing look at one another.

Even better, you'll find that many of those people will take it upon themselves to get up, come over, and tell you just how fabulous your hair is!

REASON #5: Nappturous hair is touchable! You can touch your hair! That's right! No worries about rock hard styles, curls that must stay perfectly arranged, or any of those other styling concerns! You may have to train yourself to keep your own hands out of your hair; your loving relationship with your hair will be so irresistible!

With Sisterlock™ wearers, the term is "hands-in-the-hair-itis"! Caution: You'll also notice that your hair will attract many other hands too – some that you know, and many that you don't!

REASON #6: Individuality! Look around. Who else looks exactly like you with your nappturous crown? Exactly. No one. The individuality of your hair is customizable in so many different ways!

The ultimate confidence comes from being the original person that you were created to be! Your styling ability develops with time and becomes uniquely yours.

REASON #7: A New Relationship is Developed. If you've been Nappturous for at least two or more years, you probably have experienced a little known secret about our hair and not even known it. This secret is that you now have a relationship with your hair.

Close your eyes for me and think back to the minutes, hours and sometimes full length days that you sat in the hair salon…remember? I have friends that would take breakfast, lunch and dinner with them to the salon; they would be there literally all day! Not to say that there's anything wrong with sitting around, reading every single Black Hair magazine and smelling the fragrance of hot curlers on just-relaxed hair, but doesn't the freedom from only a few select individuals being able to do your hair feel good?

Now, you still may go to the salon for the recommended trim and deep condition when you're Nappturous, and you may even have a regular appointment. But the freedom comes with knowing that you now have a positive relationship with your hair.

You've stood in front of the mirror, curling, twisting, and spritzing with water your nappturous hair for hours, and you know what side or patch is curlier, straighter, or longer than the other.

You have the freedom of knowing what styles look good on you, and also trying new styles, knowing that you can change them yourself with greater ease. Chances are, if you had to do your hair yourself, you could, and you most likely do on a regular basis.

REASON #8: You are the NEW Trendsetter! Have you ever been a trendsetter? If you have nappturous hair, I want you to stop right now and count the number of people who have become natural hair wearers as a result of your influence.

Did you ever think your mother, or another black female close to you, would actually approve of your hair…to the point where she decided to become natural? Now look at her, loving the life and freedom of nappturosity!

REASON #9: Nappturous Divas can tell you the ups and downs of almost any product! We have redefined, relabeled and upgraded the term 'product junkie'! The ability to read a label and actually know the good from the bad ingredients has transcended our hair and is now applied to almost everything else, from personal care products to even the foods we eat.

When you become aware of the health and life of your hair, you become aware of the health and life of all things around you. A respect for healthy living is developed, plus, people now come to you for product advice!

REASON #10: Love abounds. When you discover the nappturosity of your own hair, how beautiful, sexy and fabulous it is, you can look at others with admiration without feeling jealousy or resentment.

It's ok – almost everyone has gone through a stage of wishing that their hair looked like someone else's. However, the love-relationship you develop as you appreciate your own God-given beauty, the soft velvety-sheen of your hair, the way that it looks in that particular style – it's pure joy!

Nappturous Diva's Principle #1 - RELATIONSHIP

We Develop a Relationship with Our Hair

We have a plan for our hair, and we listen to what our hair needs and find solutions for challenges. Caring for our hair becomes a ritual and we use that time to assess what is working and what is not. We're flexible!

Isn't it a good feeling when you really know someone? You can anticipate their next words and you don't have to worry about formalities. In short, you've reached a certain comfort level that only comes with time.

The amazing relationship that we should have with our hair sometimes develops when we're adults, because many of us have no recollection of our original texture. Even the new growth that you develop in the first few months after making the decision to become natural is not a good indication of what your true hair texture is like.

Getting to a familiar place with your hair requires the same patience and time, and comes with personal experience.

Your relationship with your hair will change as your life changes. You'll mature and start graying, start exercising more, cut your hair down to a short afro or grow your locs long, and each one of these examples of change exemplifies a situation where being in a positive relationship with your hair will help you to know how to adjust. You'll need to be flexible. You'll need to have a plan.

The most important thing that you can do to develop this relationship with your hair is to begin with the end in mind. Crafting your goals ahead of time allows you to directly influence your results. Wouldn't it be great to know where you want to be and exactly how you're going to get there, all while allowing room for freedom and flexibility?

2

developingtheplan

To have fun and be productive in crafting your goals, the first step we will take in developing a relationship with your hair is to help you implement the Nappturous Diva's PPP Approach, or Plan, Prepare, and Pamper Approach.

Different transitions bring a multitude of different questions and considerations, and being prepared for that will help you in the long run! The PPP Approach helps you to take a "right-now" assessment of your hair, whether you've been natural for years or are just thinking about it. It is helpful

to know the "why" behind what you are doing and determine where you want to go from there.

To begin, think about what you would do if you decided you were going to treat yourself to a well-deserved vacation. You might put together a plan for a special evening, prepare the arrangements that you need to make it happen and then engage yourself in pampering activities, all the while thinking about how much fun you'll have. All of your thoughts would probably fall into one of three categories – Planning, Preparing or Pampering.

It's good to realize that how you choose to PPP for a vacation might not be how someone else chooses to – but at the end of the time invested, you both have accomplished the same goal. You've relaxed and gotten to know yourself a little better.

The PPP Approach to hair follows the same common sense rules as in developing self-confidence. There is a direct correlation between someone who feels relaxed and confident about their hair and the level of development of their relationship with their hair and knowing what works for them. There will be many influencers weighing in on what you should do, but the person who determines the exact method and means in the end is you.

As we develop your personalized PPP Approach together, it's important to realize that you'll need to incorporate acceptance, practicality and honesty into goals and evaluations of the progress of your hair.

For example, if you grew up with kinky hair, and you want to be chemical free, no amount of natural product will change the fact that your hair is kinky. The same flowing fro you may have seen on entertainer and singer Kelis might be a realistic goal for you, or it might not. As you are empowered with education on your options and different ways to achieve your goals dependent upon your hair texture, you'll be able to draft a better PPP Approach.

Before we go any further, have you thought about your reasons for wanting to undertake the transitions that come along with creating and maintaining natural hair? The transitions bring certain changes along with it, that, if you aren't sure why you are natural, you won't be able to stick with it.

A common misconception is that the only major transition occurs when going from relaxed to natural hair. However, there is a substantial transition experienced by transitioning to locs from natural hair as well, and many more transitions that occur as you age and your lifestyle changes.

What does having natural hair or locs mean to you, and why do you want to make this commitment?

Common Reasons to have and maintain the Natural Hair Decision

Style: Trends go around and around, and as my mother would say, there's nothing new under the sun. Let's be real – it has become popular to have natural hair. For some people, this is the only reason they need to make the decision to go natural, and if that's you, that's fine.

You value uniqueness and expression. Using style to express your sense of being through your hair gives you many options, and your look will be your own. Even the same style will look different on you than on someone else!

Questions to consider: Are you going to still want natural hair if it becomes less trendy? How will being natural now affect any future trends that you may want to follow?

Health: Have you broken the "creamy crack" or "chemical fire cream" addiction to relaxers? Are you sick and tired of a burning scalp and hair loss? Did you cringe when you realized that the average ph of relaxers is between 12 and 14, far above the safe recommended ph of hair products of 4-6? The definition of natural hair is hair that has not been permanently altered by any type of chemical.

Making a change for health reasons allows you to experience a "two-for-one" success in the areas of both your health and your hair. You'll find that the commitment to go natural for health reasons soon becomes holistic, spreading to other areas of your life.

An ingredient reader of a hair product soon becomes an ingredient reader of food and other products!

Questions to consider: For you, does natural hair translate into natural living? What other routes are you willing to consider supporting the decision to be natural for health reasons? i.e. Supplements, increasing water intake, etc.

Cultural Aspects and/or Spirituality: You've decided to become natural because it aligns with your current mantra of incorporating an awareness of your cultural or spiritual identity in all that you do. It reflects a deeper level of consciousness and connects you to the spiritual realm.

For you, being natural is more than a hairstyle; it's a lifestyle and a platform for you to inspire those who ask you about your hair.

You also may want to make a statement to those who have oppressed your sense of who you were created to be and help those who want to follow in your example. Making a statement allows you to identify with others who have similar beliefs.

Questions to consider: What impression do you want to leave on those who ask "uneducated questions" about your hair? Does your current lifestyle accommodate your choice of cultural expression?

Versatility: With natural hair, you can truly have it "your way!" Long gone is the myth that natural hair can only accommodate certain styles.

Many natural sisters are finding that healthier hair lends to increased versatility and styling options! When your hair is natural, you don't feel as limited as you may have thought you would before your transition, and you have more room to experiment with your hair.

An added bonus is that if you choose to wear more protective styles, you'll protect your length, which equates into even more styling options.

Questions to consider: Will you be able to achieve the look you want with natural hair? Will you need extra classes or coaching on styling to achieve the different styles you want? Where will you obtain that assistance?

Freedom: Did wearing your hair in its pre-natural style feel like you were sentenced to 30 years at the corner salon, complete with a sweet potato pie lady and cd bootlegger? If you have locs, maybe you just wanted to be able to go for a week without worrying about how your hair would be styled.

If you transitioned from a relaxer to a natural style, did you ever think twice about whether your relaxed curls were going to drop when the humidity hit? Natural hair and locs do provide a certain sense of independence, especially when you begin maintaining your hair personally.

Questions to consider: What coping mechanism will you use to commit to the initial few months of learning your hair texture and/or necessary maintenance? How much freedom do you want?

Your reasons might be a combination of the ones listed above, and may even include a few that are not listed. Before we go any further, express your feelings by drafting your reasons why you feel this option is the one for you.

My Why Statement:

I (have natural hair/want to be natural/have locs/want to make this transition) because:

You may have chosen one or more reasons for your commitment for your hair from the list provided earlier, or even added reasons not listed. It is not likely that your Why Statement will be exactly like someone else's. Being confident in your reasons allows you to embrace and support others who have chosen nappturosity for reasons unlike yours. What we look like, act like and how we treat others is simply a reflection of our own self-confidence, and internal knowledge of the reason why we have chosen our particular route. Your knowledge allows you to shine and gives permission to others around you to shine as well!

Things you can do to prepare yourself for a transition:

- Talk to other people who have a similar hair texture and look that you want

- Search the internet for support groups and message boards that flow with your goals and philosophy, starting with the list included in this book

- Look for and collect pictures of where you want your hair to be, we'll use them later in the development of your personalized PPP approach

- If needed, use the section of the book on how to research and interview hair stylists to find one that makes you completely comfortable and has the skills and stability to help you reach your goals

- Complete the **Nappturosity: How to Create Fabulous Natural Hair and Locs** PPP Approach and Natural Hair Manifesto in the following section, then come back in a year and notate all of the goals that have been accomplished! If you know where you've begun, you're able to make a more fair assessment of what you've achieved! Be proud of your results!

Back In The Day...

I remember when I began to commit myself to my own PPP Approach. I read everything that I could find on the topic of being natural, talked to people I knew and used their encouragement as inspiration. Like most women who are natural, I wanted to be proud of my hair and also feel confident about my abilities to make it work for me.

I began with a lot of mis-information, and that made the journey harder. Like many women, I was impatient with my hair, and didn't really craft out the investment of time needed, yet was disappointed when it wasn't developing the way I wanted it to develop.

My number one goal was healthy hair.

My number two goal was length.   These were two things that never previously occurred simultaneously with my natural hair. By honestly evaluating and appreciating my kinky, dense, fragile and coarse 3C, 4A & 4B texture, and wanting to commit to doing the greatest good for my hair and myself, I determined that the fastest way for me to reach these goals at the same time would be to loc my hair, which was a major transition for me, with both challenging and enjoyable times.

Over the years I've updated my PPP Approach annually, and every year, I'm excited about watching my hair develop as planned. If you can honestly look at what you're starting with, and give yourself permission to love your own hair, you'll experience better results faster.

creatingyourcustomPPPapproach

Step #1: Plan

Every beautiful result began with a plan. A written plan helps you to realize your goals 90% faster.

This concept also applies to your hair. We will first assess where you are, then draft your dream

goals and use this information to craft your own Natural Hair Manifesto! Every good plan began

with questions, so pull out a pen and let's get started!

Assess Where You Are:

1.   What is the current condition of your hair?

2.   Have you recently transitioned from a relaxer to natural hair?

3.   Have you recently transitioned from loose natural hair to locs?

4.   Have you recently transitioned from locs to loose natural hair?

5.   What other transitions are you approaching?

6.   Do you like to or want to color your hair?

7.   How often do you go to a salon or stylist for maintenance?

8.   What's your current budget for hair maintenance and products?

9.   Are there any aspects about your health that would affect your hair?   Medication, Exercise, Swimming?

10. If you enjoy your lifestyle, are there any other activities you would do more frequently if you had more flexible hairstyle?

11. Do you currently take any supplements to help your hair internally?

12. Are you getting enough water daily?

13. How do you currently feel about your hair?

Dream Goals

Dream a little, and determine where you would like to be in a year:

Now, let's convert those dreams into specific, measurable, achievable goals for the next 12 months.

Using the dream you've written as inspiration, we will draft the plan section of your personalized PPP approach.

My Natural Hair Manifesto

12-Month Goals

In twelve months, I want:

1. The condition of my hair to be:

2. The budget for hair maintenance and products to be:

3. To go to the salon how often:

4. To participate in the following health related activities that affect my hair:

5. To feel the following way about my hair:

6.   To describe my hair with these 3 words:

The Action Steps

To manifest these goals, I will:

1.   Condition of My hair:

    a.   What do I need to do to make my goal in #1 happen? List as many points here as needed.

2.   Investment of time and money:

    a. What do I need to do to make my goal in #2 & #3 happen? List as many points here as needed.

3.   Health Related Activities that Affect My Hair:

    a. What do I need to do to make #4 happen? List as many points here as needed.

4.   Feelings About My hair:

    a. What do I need to do to make #5 happen? List as many points here as needed.

Congratulations! You've completed one of the most important steps to creating fabulous natural hair and locs! You have a clear, guiding intention that will allow you to make the best choices in your hair care so that you can achieve your goals in the most expeditious manner.

What you focus on manifests, so you'll be able to refer to this Natural Hair Manifesto when you are going through any number of transitions with your hair to keep you in line with what matters most to you.

Step #2: Prepare

The preparation step takes your goals and manifestos and prepares them for real world application. In this step, we will examine areas that could possibly prevent your goals from manifesting – Opinions, Negative Reinforcement, and Wishful Thinking. Solutions to these potential issues will be presented in the form of Possibility Statements.

Opinions

There is one absolute that I will guarantee you: As soon as you determine in your mind that you are going to make your chosen transition, it is likely that someone will call your decision into question. Their comments, maybe even shared in love, may cause you to second guess the Natural Hair Manifesto that we just created.

Being that we live in a world that, 24 hours a day, reinforces its own perspective on how we should think, feel or wear our hair, you'll find that the most reliable answer to the resource that you need to make the transition to natural hair or to locs is YOU and your own educated opinion.

You already possess the consciousness.

You already possess the answers. You may need to do a little in-depth thought processing to encourage the answers you need to manifest. By focusing on the positive words and thoughts, you begin directing instead of being directed.

You may have heard so much negativity about natural hair over your lifetime that it seems normal to you to speak negative words over your head or the heads of others. The words you use powerfully determine the actions that you take.

They can destroy self-esteem, damage goals and stunt your growth as you progress towards your goals.

I encourage you to make an effort to be aware of how you talk about yourself and your dreams, as well as whom you talk to about those items as well.

Take a moment and think about the damaging phrases that you've heard about natural hair or locs and identify the ones that you can honestly say that you have thought, even if only for a moment.

Negative Reinforcement & Wishful Thinking

- "My hair is just not healthy enough to go natural."

- "I could never wear my hair like that."

- "Locs are dirty. It must be hard to keep them clean."

- "Natural hair requires too much work."

- "I could never attract a relationship with that kind of hair."

- "My job just wouldn't accept me with my hair like that."

- "I wish my hair would do that."

- "My new growth is just too thick; I couldn't manage it without a relaxer."

- "People who have locs are militant."

- "My hair should be further along than it is right now!"

- "I'll always have (fill in the blank) hair!"

- "I don't think that my hair would look right like that."

- "That style works for her, but it would never work for me because my _____ is too _____!"

- Add a few of your own:
    - 1.

    - 2.

    - 3.

Are there any thoughts that you have identified? These thoughts or sayings need to be replaced by empowering words.

Do you believe that if you had more extensive experience or education about natural hair and locs, that you wouldn't have circled any of the statements above?   Prepare yourself for your transition by choosing to have empowering thoughts.

The idea does not suggest that you should pretend like everything is perfect, because it may not be. However, by developing a positive position in your thinking and speaking, you remain open to the possibility of your goals being attained.

Turn those self-deprecating thoughts or ideas into statements that make room for possibility by going through the following two stages and creating empowering beliefs.

Possibility Statement - Stage One

State the idea that you are working on changing from a negative to a positive; add a "but", and then state the positive outcome. Here are a few examples of what I mean:

- "My hair may not be healthy right now, **but** through proper maintenance, I believe I can develop a head of lush, healthy hair!

- "The people at my place of employment may initially wonder what I did to my hair, **but** they will get used to it and accept me as I am."

- "I used to wish my hair would have the texture of hers, **but** I have learned that every type of hair has challenges and celebrations, and I will celebrate my texture."

- "I used to believe that my relationships were based on how I wear my hair, **but** now I choose to be with someone who accepts me totally and completely, natural hair and all!"

This is a very small, easy transition to make in your speaking. Again, when you find yourself making a negative statement, stop and make the necessary adjustment!

Once you surpass this level, you are ready for…

Possibility Statement - Stage Two

Using the 12 Month Goals from your Natural Hair Manifesto, state those 12 Month Goals as though they are happening *right now!* You may not see the physical change, but you know that if you've stated your goal and you're taking the proper action as detailed on your Manifesto, the change *is* occurring!

When you think about your hair, as in the morning when you're getting ready for your day and looking in the mirror, smile and say, "The condition of my hair is becoming softer and full of luster and sheen. I love the way my scalp feels so much healthier, and the style I have is a great complement to my features." When you state the ultimate goal as though it is happening at this very moment, you are literally *creating* your present and future outcomes, deepening your confidence and showering yourself with healthy self-love!

Thoughts plus words equal actions. As you change your thoughts, begin to watch the reactions of those around you change. Embrace your natural texture, love the way that **your** hair grows and develops!

Prepare yourself by empowering yourself to speak your goals with complete belief, and you'll soon see others echoing your sentiments. Email me and let me know when that happens! I want to know and share your testimony with others!

Information for preparation will come your way through this book and other forms of media, and when they do, choose the ones that will best prepare you for the achievement of your desires.

In-House Expert! Kaya Casper, Publisher of Naturally You! Magazine

On "The Celebrations and Challenges of Natural Hair"

Naturally You! Magazine was founded by Kaya Casper in 2003, in response to a lack of information in print magazines for women who choose to wear their hair 100% naturally. Naturally You! is the first magazine to focus on natural hair care, without the use of chemicals or added hair. Naturally You! Magazine's mission is to empower Black women around the world by providing reliable and current information on natural hair care, beauty, and holistic health and wellness. www.naturallyyoumagazine.com

What are the top 3 reasons we should celebrate having natural hair?

Reason one, I would say that our hair is very versatile. I think sometimes when we have a relaxer and are straightening our hair we don't realize all the versatility that we have in our natural hair. We can wear braids, twists, we can loc our hair, we can wear a fro, we can wear a million and one textured styles, we can wear it short and long-- there's just so much we can do with our natural hair.

Reason two, its one of the best gifts that we have received, and it is straight from God. We were born that way. It's a hair type that is actually admired by a variety of different cultures, and it's time that we join other people in appreciating what we have. As human beings in general, we don't appreciate what we have naturally, and its time that we start doing that. Reason three, accepting our natural hair is a part of overall self-acceptance, and if we do that we can do so much.

You've been the publisher of Naturally You! Magazine since 2003 – what changes in the natural hair community have you seen since then?

For one, the natural community has really grown! It came from a very small segment of the population to the point where now, when you turn on the TV you see a handful of women with natural hair everyday. When I walk down the street here in Philly, I see more advertisements with women with natural hair, more so than women with straight hair. Even walking down the street I see more women with natural hair and that's something I didn't see in 1997 when I first went natural or in 2003 when I began Naturally You! Magazine. In major cities there's been a huge increase in the number of women with natural hair, but also, the scope of people with natural hair has changed a lot. It's gone from being just for people who are different, artistic or on the cutting edge to something a lot of people are doing for a lot of different reasons, sometimes just because they like the hairstyle. In a lot of ways it's become mainstream, which I wouldn't say that that's a bad thing.

What are some of the perceived challenges with natural hair and locs?

The most common misconception is that natural hair is difficult to care for; another thing is people associate it with a very negative stigma. A lot of times people think it's impossible to comb, extremely dry, hard to the touch, or extremely coarse. As far as the negative perceptions, people think it's unprofessional and not lady-like-- they won't be able to get a man or a job. Even with locs, people are going to think I'm going to be dirty and that I don't wash my hair, which is just really sad to me. The remedies for that are just learning, doing the research and talking to people who have natural hair. There are a lot of resources online now, whereas 10 years ago there weren't. Even if you don't have Internet access, there are books out there. Even coming down to just walking up to people who have natural hair and asking them questions-- that's going to best for breaking out of the misconceptions of challenges of having natural hair.

Your magazine, of course, is a source of both entertainment and education within the natural hair community. Why do you think continuing that education is important?

I think it is really important to educate ourselves as much as possible. It does a lot to expand our horizons and allows us to understand things on a bigger scale, and natural hair is no exception. Unfortunately, a lot of us have been perming our hair since we were little girls and can't go to our mothers to ask for that information. They've been perming our hair since we were little girls, they've been perming their hair since they were little girls, so we need to go to the books and Internet and read Naturally You! Magazine and ask others who have natural hair. That's what is going to allow us to break out of the negative perceptions, the lack of self-acceptance and really move forward.

Step #3: Pamper

Now that you have completed the first two steps, Plan and Prepare, you can use the tips here to turn your hair time into a little piece of heaven in an otherwise busy, filled day. Pampering is not about investing a lot of time into a routine, it is about doing what YOUR hair needs. Pampering will help you to achieve hair goals faster! The more educated you are about your hair; the less time is needed, because you'll know what works for you.

This book has been designed to turn that mentality around by providing the latest, most efficient information for you to achieve what I call "hair peace."

Don't you deserve a little pampering? Let's find out. Check off all that apply to you.

Have you ever:

o Rushed through detangling after washing, only to discover that the teeth of the comb broke somewhere within your new growth?

o Gone for longer than one month without conditioning your hair?

o Wondered what was in the product you were using, but chose to use it anyway because it "smelled so good!"?

o Decided in the middle of an at-home hair session that doing your natural hair was too hard and immediately picked up your phone and scheduled an appointment for braids?

o Cried or felt badly about the state or condition of your hair?

o Been told by your stylist or really honest friend that you had "see-through" hair (hair that hasn't been trimmed in ages)?

o Swept up enough hair off the floor to make a wig?

o Worn a wig because you were having a "bad hair day"?

o Slapped a texturizer or relaxer in your hair in frustration after a few months trying to be natural, only to regret it later?

If you are kind to your hair, your hair will reward you! Invest in the proper supplies, products and support that you need for your hair type. If you're just getting started and you've never done your own hair a day in your life, you may need the support of a stylist more frequently than someone who is more experienced. That's ok! If you have thin edges or hair that is taking a longer time to form mature locs, you'll have to retighten or conduct loc maintenance more often than some others. That's ok too!

Realize where you are and what you need, and before you know it, your Natural Hair Manifesto will begin to come to fruition. Pampering requires you to slow down, relax, and is based on a more gentle touch. Pampering also requires an organized system to reduce your investment and time.

As you learn and apply new techniques, you'll be able to do what is necessary for healthy hair growth and enjoy yourself throughout the process.

The Process of Pampering

First, gather all of your products, ingredients and supplies, and clear a special shelf in your bathroom or closet for them. Place everything that you need for your hair here, and make this area the official home of your hair supplies.

Consider adding a few additional items that will relax and help you enjoy the time even more. Some favorite pampering tools that Nappturous Divas have been known to use during their sacred hair time include motivational cd's, jazz, hip-hop and spa music, candles, special oils, empowering magazines, books and hot tea. What you choose depends on how much time you want to spend on your hair. For longer time periods – twenty minutes or more – you may want to ask a loved one to help with any little loved ones, and retreat into your space. Do your thing!

Can you picture it? Let me assist you in envisioning a perfect hair pampering moment. How does this sound…

It's Saturday morning about 7am, before everyone wakes up. The sun is rising and warm orange light is jetting across the dim sky. You heat up a pot of tea, place it on a tray and carry it to your hair space. The rosemary mint candle gently wafts an invigorating fragrance throughout the room, and the soft flame greets you from beside your bathtub. As you wet your hair and gently massage in your pre-shampoo treatment, you then take a bath and shampoo your hair afterwards. After applying conditioner, you sip tea and read a book that lifts your mood and your spirit. Upon rinsing the conditioner out, you rinse again with your clarifying treatment and then moisturize with your leave-in conditioner. Detangling is a breeze since proper conditioning has taken place, and, after an optional twisting, your hair is ready to air dry! All of your hair tools go back to their home and your hair is fresh, rejuvenated and smelling wonderful, and you're ready to start your day!

Despite your chosen time investment, you will benefit by designating at least one day a month to recreate this perfect moment.

For all of the other times when that perfect moment cannot be created, you can still incorporate some regular pampering routines into your schedule. Try these tips to optimize your time:

- Keep your hair supplies in a shower organizer or near the area where you care for your hair

- If you only have time for a quick shampoo, add a conditioning agent to the shampoo for added moisture. A simple teaspoon of olive oil combined with a handful of shampoo adds extra conditioning!

- Set a regular day and time for your hair care routine, preferably during a time where you are least likely to be rushed or interrupted.

- Wash your hair, add your conditioner and put on a conditioning cap before bathing. Rinse your hair at the end of your bath. You'll experience even better results when showering, because the steam opens the hair cuticle and allows moisture to be better absorbed!

By committing yourself to pampering, you'll also communicate an important message to yourself and to any little ones who are watching, that your hair is a part of you that you treasure, respect and believe is an asset. The messages you give off help others to understand how to better value you, and aid them in developing their own self-esteem and sense of pride in themselves as well!

4

basicmaintenance:
what's a hair care regime?

New Naturals and Transitioners often ask me exactly what they need to do to care for their hair, especially when it comes to how often to shampoo, condition and moisturize. Finding the regime that works for you is more of an art than an exact science. Note that the regime that works for your best girlfriend or favorite celebrity may not work for you! Everyone's hair is slightly different and the information you need is just that – a guide to point you in the right direction to achieve your personal hair goals and do what works best for your hair condition and type.

The ideal hair care regime consists of knowing exactly how you will rotate through the steps of your regular hair care routine, and can include the following seven steps: pre-shampoo, shampoo set, shampoo or no-poo, condition, clarify, detangle, and moisturize.

For the best results with curly, wavy or kinky afro textured hair, *the first 6 steps of this regime should be conducted no more than every 5-7 days. The only exception is rinsing the hair and/or using the pre-shampoo treatment to rid your hair of sweat or chlorine, or to moisturize it for styling.*

We start with the **pre-shampoo, also called a pre-poo treatment**. A pre-poo treatment helps your hair receive moisture before going into a shampoo, which can sometimes be drying. A pre-poo treatment also reduces time spent later in the detangling stage, resulting in less hair loss, and shields your hair against the harsh detergents that are in the majority of store bought shampoos. It is extremely beneficial for those who have hard, dry or easily tangled hair and also softens the tresses.

Step #1 – Pre Shampoo/Pre-Poo

Wet your hair thoroughly with a sprayer or under the faucet. Apply your pre-poo treatment evenly throughout your hair. Use of a thicker, heavier conditioner is fine because of the multiple rinses that will be conducted throughout the routine. If you have locs, always use a natural oil, like olive or castor oil, or a light-weight conditioner for your pre-poo. <u>Do not</u> rinse before moving to the next step.

Step #2 – Shampoo Set

Second is the **shampoo set**. This step is optional, but very important for those who are working on maintaining length, transitioning from a relaxer, have new locs, a scalp or dandruff problem or have hair that is easily tangled or prone to breakage. In the shampoo set, you'll divide your hair into about 16 sections and loosely braid each section, with the pre-poo treatment still in your hair. The shampoo set will help you to preserve the health of your hair without subjecting it to the harsh friction of shampooing, and allow you to have clearer access to your scalp. On average, we loose about 50-100 hairs a day! Thankfully, these hairs are routinely replaced with new hairs, but outside of this normal shedding, why not keep all the hair you can?

Whether you have locs, natural hair or are transitioning, investing the time in this step will make you a 'believer' in the shampoo set when you don't see the huge accumulation of hair in the sink after your routine is over!

To begin, divide your hair into four sections with your fingers, clip the remaining sections, and divide the one you are now working with into four sections.

Gently comb the hair in one section from the ends down to the root with a large-tooth comb. Loosely braid the section, and move on to the next one. Continue this process with each section and when you're done, you will have a total of sixteen loose braids.

This method helps to reduce the friction from scrubbing your hair, and helps to get the product directly to the scalp when you shampoo. If your hair is too short to braid, putting a hair net over your hair and then shampooing will achieve similar results.

Braiding is optional, and this step can be incorporated as a protective measure.

Step #3 – Shampoo/Poo

Third, you'll need to decide how to handle a new, revolutionary question…to poo, or not to poo?

Shampooing the hair used to be the next logical step, but many natural hair wearers are choosing to wash their hair with conditioner, thus creating the "no-poo" option

What is the No-Poo Technique? Who wouldn't use shampoo to wash their hair? Actually, a lot of people! This method has existed for a while, and has achieved recent popularity as more and more people are using the No-Poo Technique with beautiful results. Simply put, the No-Poo

Technique consists of washing your hair using conditioner instead of shampoo. No-pooing is a great method to use in between shampoos for a quick rinse of the hair and scalp after exercising or when wetting your hair to re-style.

Through no-pooing, you'll notice softer, more manageable hair, and a shorter time spent detangling and getting in and out of the shower or bathtub to shampoo, rinse, apply conditioner and then rinse again.

Contrary to my initial belief, I have found that this method still results in clean hair. If you still feel you must shampoo and wash your hair with a gentle shampoo, you will do well alternating between pooing and no-pooing weekly, or using a diluted version of your current shampoo, especially if you have dry hair.

Using the shampoo or conditioner of choice, spread the product first on the roots of the hair, extending out towards the ends of the hair. Use your palm and fingertips to massage your scalp and hair gently, in circular motions. This helps your circulation, and increases blood flow to the scalp, which stimulates hair growth.

You can gently rub the exposed areas of the scalp and allow your fingers to go through the base of your loose braids, washing your hair thoroughly. Rinse from the roots to the tips of each braid at least twice. If you skipped that step, using your fingers, part the hair and rinse the scalp thoroughly, to the ends of your hair.

Nappturous Diva Breaks It Down: Understanding the ph of Products

The ph of a product is rated on a scale of 0-14, and determines how acidic or alkaline it is. Acidic ingredients, like lemon juice (ph=2.2) and vinegar (ph=3) contract the hair shaft, while alkaline ingredients like ammonia (ph=12) break down the hair shaft. The natural ph of our skin is between 4.6-6, and products that remain in that range are most conducive to the health of our hair. For example, a relaxer, a.k.a. texturizer, a.k.a. silkener, is formulated to permanently alter the structural composition of your hair, and accomplishes that goal by using chemicals that "soften" or break down the hair shaft. Don't be deceived by the gentle verbiage relaxer manufacturers use! The process of relaxing your hair actually mimics an actual chemical fire taking place on your scalp and hair!

Step #4 - Condition

Fourth, **conditioning** the hair is particularly important if your hair is colored, or prone to dryness or breakage.

Generously spread your conditioner of choice throughout the sections of your hair and then cover with a conditioning cap for 15-30 minutes, or sit under a steamer if available. **Deep condition** your hair by leaving the cap on for at least 30-60 minutes under the steamer. Do not rinse until the end of Step Five.

Step #5 - Detangle

If you incorporated the shampoo set, gently **detangle** your hair one braid at a time with your fingers. If not, still detangle your hair one section at a time. Once your hair is separated, use the wide-tooth comb or Denman D3 brush gently from ends to roots to further detangle.

If this is your first time following Steps One through Five, you'll probably discover that your hair is much softer and easier to detangle than it has ever been. By detangling one braid or section at a time, your hair will stay wet longer, and wet hair that is saturated with conditioner is easier to detangle than dry hair. Be patient and gentle during this stage.

You'll most likely be surprised with how little hair is left in the comb or brush, or on the sink and the floor, and you'll know that you're on your way to really maintaining the ends of your hair and seeing length faster. Overall, your hair will simply be healthier!

Rinse your hair for at least 2 minutes with cool water, which allows the cuticle, or outer layer of the hair strand, to close and retain more of the moisture that has been applied.

Step #6 - Clarify

Now on to the sixth, optional, **clarifying** step. Rinsing your hair with a clarifying treatment helps to reduce both product buildup and dry scalp/dandruff! Using the treatment, pour or spray a third over your hair, concentrating on the scalp, and gently massage your scalp for two minutes.

Without rinsing, continue with the second third of the treatment, and massage for two minutes again. Finish with the last third of the clarifier; massage for two minutes and then rinse your hair with water if necessary. This step should be conducted a minimum of once a month or as needed.

Nappturous Diva Breaks It Down: Where Does Product Build-Up Come From, and What Can I do About It?

Conditioners, silicones, styling aids and wax-based products are all formulated to coat the hair. When too many of these products are applied over a period of time, the deposits that they leave on your hair are called build-up. What's the problem with build-up? In order for the natural sebum that your skin produces to be distributed through your hair, your scalp needs to breathe!

Product build-up clogs the hair follicles, leading to dry scalp and dandruff concerns, and usually cannot be removed by rinsing alone!

How do you know if you have product buildup?

Look for residue under your fingernail after you gently scratch your scalp, and also take note of a dull appearance of your hair or lack of sheen. Using a basic hair clarifying treatment containing baking soda, lemon juice, apple cider vinegar or other simple, natural preparation will safely and gently remove product buildup and leave you with an amazingly bright sheen and clean hair and scalp!

Step #7 - Moisturize

The seventh and last step is **moisturizing**. Adding moisture is nourishment to both your hair and scalp. Thankfully, we have evolved from the thick, mineral oil based greases and creams to lighter, more natural products that add real moisture to the hair and scalp.

These products include sprays and creams and are classified under names you may recognize, such as leave-in conditioner, as well as names that may make you a little hungry, including hair milk, hair teas, hair soufflé and hair milkshakes!

Hair oils should be used in a moisturizing product, or after moisturizing to lubricate and seal the dampness in the hair, helping to retain the moisture that has been applied.

Use a super-absorbent hair towel to soak up excess water from the hair, while your hair is still damp; use your fingers and separate hair into large sections, applying the moisturizing products of choice.

With the same sections, braid or flat twist the hair, applying more water on sections that may have dried, and your hair is now ready to air dry. Braiding helps immensely, especially if you're going to be sleeping on your hair! This allows the hair to stay detangled and separated and makes it easier to style later on. Another option is to skip the braiding step and allow your hair to air-dry. If you've used a curl enhancing moisturizer, wait until the hair is dry to separate the curls and style with your fingers.

Loc wearers should go through their hair and separate locs that may be clinging to each other at the base – always do this when your hair is wet instead of dry! Now is a great time to apply rollers, twists or otherwise style your locs, so that it sets and air-dries at the same time.

I repeat, always, always, always air-dry your hair when possible!

You'll find the Nappturous Diva's homemade and commercial recommendations in the products section of this book. To know how often to moisturize, look for telltale signs that your hair needs moisture, such as a dry, brittle texture, extra frizz, or routine breakage, and use moderate amounts of the moisturizing product regularly to keep these issues at bay!

On average, use a moisturizing product from the root to tip of the hair a minimum of 3 times a week.

Nappturous Diva's Personal Weekly Hair Care Regime*

Over the years, I have learned to respond to my hair when it needs extra care, and I must admit, I had to learn the hard way!

Realizing that my lifestyle is the major factor that influences my regime – which is why everyone's regime will be slightly different – I customized this plan to scale. For example, during the summer, we participate in a lot of outdoor events, and I have to take precautions against dry hair with the level of heat in my area. Therefore, my summer regime consists of extra steps that promote moisture and elasticity. You'll find the scrumptious recipes I use detailed in full later on in this book!

Pre-Poo: Soaking my hair thoroughly, I divide my locs into sections and gently massage a few handfuls of 100% Pure Castor Oil from scalp to tip, allowing to condition for 15-30 minutes. I leave this treatment on my hair and move to the next step.

Shampoo: I then use a 1:5 dilution of Dr. Bronner's Peppermint Shampoo and shampoo my hair twice, rinsing thoroughly.

Condition: Once a month, I use the Sweetness Condish*. I gently rub the mixture through my locs, cover and let sit for an hour.

Clarify: Warm Sweetness Hair & Scalp Treatment* leaves my locs clarified and conditioned! Because I exercise almost daily, I do this step every week to rinse my scalp thoroughly.

Moisturize: I then separate my locs at the root, and evenly distribute Karen's Body Beautiful Hair Milk or Sisterlocks™ Moisture Treatment throughout my locs, and seal with a small amount of jojoba oil. I reapply every 2-3 days, increasing that to a light coating daily during the summer!

Loc Freshener: Bed-head is no more! I used to detest the flatness of my hair after waking and the "outdoors" or "food" fragrance my locs would pick up whenever I went outside or cooked. I spritz with the lovely scented Bed-head Growth Spray* daily to condition and freshen my locs.

*Nappturous Diva's homemade recipes located in Principle #3

howto**grow**strong**healthy**hair

Remember, if you want your hair and scalp to be at their healthiest, the best long-term benefits come from ensuring that our bodies are taken care of. At places ranging from churches to seminars, a popular question I am asked is "How do I grow my hair?" For many, the answer is surprising. Everyone has the ability to have healthy, strong and lengthy hair. Different styling methods optimize growth, like locs, but the root of hair growth is an internal function, not an external function. It doesn't matter how much "Doo-Gro" we use, the

outside is always a manifestation of the inside. By the way, aren't you glad that product manufacturers are realizing that we can read and spell correctly?

Hopefully these tips will serve as a reminder as well as inspiration for a healthier lifestyle! Healthy bodies increase the likelihood that our hair will be healthy as well. Develop a healthier lifestyle and healthier hair by:

1. Eating Healthy Foods: Increase your protein, fiber and whole foods intake. Consider trying more vegetable sources of protein, healthier, nitrate-free meats; heart-healthy soy and soymilk to drink or in your cooking; whole foods and whole grain breads.

Nappturous Diva Breaks It Down: My Secret for Healthy Hair Growth…Wheat Grass!

Oh, how I love wheat grass! I remember the first time I was introduced to wheat grass, I was intrigued by the concept of drinking an actual "whole food" that was also a type of grass! I wondered, "Could this really help me?"

Were some of the other foods I was eating only "half foods?" The answer, as I learned, to both questions is yes and yes!

I discovered that eating more whole foods that contain essential vitamins creates healthier hair, and as I added wheat grass and other whole foods into my diet, my hair began growing by leaps and bounds.

For example, instead of one rotation at my Sisterlocks retightenings, my consultant began doing two rotations regularly. My signature Wheatgrass Smoothie recipe follows, but first, the benefits of whole foods!

Wheatgrass is just one of many types of food in a classification named "whole foods." The benefits of whole foods for your hair and body are excellent! Whole foods are foods that undergo little to no processing and refinement. There are many different types of whole foods, including unpolished grains and organically grown fruits and vegetables.

How are whole foods different from supplements?

Other than the vitamins and minerals found in supplements, whole foods contain additional carotenoids, pigments, terpenes, chlorophyll and many more components that help your body heal itself and prevent disease…and of course, help your hair to grow!

Nappturous Diva's Signature Wheat Grass Smoothie

This Wheat Grass Smoothie uses not only wheat grass, but includes other whole foods like blueberries and banana for a nutritious, live-food treat!

1 cup of vanilla soymilk

½ cup of frozen organic blueberries
½ Banana
2 shakes of cinnamon
1 heaping tablespoon of wheat grass powder
2 tablespoons of honey or agave nectar

Blend well, adding each ingredient in the order listed above, and enjoy!

Wheat grass can be purchased at any natural foods store. Ensure that the brand you buy is not mixed with other grasses, and says 100% wheat grass on the ingredient label.

Wheat grass is a green whole food, and has what some might describe as an acquired taste, which is why we add it to natural juices. In this case, making a smoothie further disguises the taste.   If the powdered version of wheat grass is not desirable to you, another option is to take wheat grass capsules. If you decide on the wheat grass capsule, read the label to check the recommended daily dosage.

When consuming wheat grass, some people see excellent results with hair and nail growth, however, it also has other benefits:

- Wheat grass absorbs 92 of the 102 known minerals found in the soil
- High in protein, and enzymes, which have been called the catalysts of life
- Rich in vitamin A, B complex, E, C, and carotene
- High chlorophyll content – which is a powerful blood builder and purifier

- Helps neutralize toxins in the body
- **Helps eliminate dandruff**
- Aids in digestion and constipation
- Helps draw off toxins from the walls of the colon (as an implant)
- Helps wash drug and chemical deposits from the body
- Chlorophyll can be found in many other green plants, but wheat grass is one of the best because of its completeness.

Additional whole and super foods to consider:

Spirulina, kelp, blue-green algae, chlorella, flax seed, spinach, broccoli, sweet potatoes, blueberries, beans, oranges, kale and whole grains, to name a few!

2. **Water**: About 60% of our bodies is water, and how much you should drink depends on various factors, ranging from the climate you live in to how much exercise you maintain.

Generally, 8 cups a day is the average recommendation. An even more precise suggestion is to divide your body weight in half, and to drink that number in ounces daily. To ensure that you're getting enough, remember to:

- Drink 1 glass between each meal
- Drink until satisfied after exercise

- Don't wait until you're thirsty to drink water, that means that you are already dehydrated

- Flavor water with lemons or other fresh fruit and substitute for soda, sugary fruit juices and powdered drinks

3. **Exercise**: You've already heard about the benefits of 30 minutes 3-4 times a week. Bob Greene, a fitness expert, is famous for telling beginners to start exercising by just "moving more." Take the stairs, park further from the entrance, walk during lunch – whatever you do, just do it consistently!

4. **Supplements**: Supplement your meals with nutrition they may not include. Look for a multi-vitamin that has a quick absorption rate. Also consider adding a hair, skin and nail vitamin to your multivitamin regime for even better results. With a multitude of options on the market, I took a brief survey of clients and friends who reported great results from the following brands:

Multivitamin:

- **Melaleuca Vitality Pack** – Very popular because of affordability and the higher than average absorption rate.

Hair, Skin & Nails Vitamins:

- **Phyto Phytophanere Dietary Supplement** - Hair & Nails Hair Fortifying Vitamins
- **Healthy Hair, Skin and Nails** by Andrew Lessman
- **Country Life High Potency Biotin** - This formulation is considered to be more pure because it contains no yeast, corn, wheat, soy, gluten, milk, salt, sugar, starch, preservatives or artificial color.

5. **Reducing Stimulants:** We might love that great café mocha or cup of coffee from our local coffee shop every morning, but consider purchasing a non-caffeinated option if you must drink coffee.

Additionally, reduce alcohol intake and increase Vitamin B, Omega 3's and sleep. Reducing the intake of both coffee and alcohol will probably save you more money…which you can use to buy more hair products!

6. **Reducing Toxic Exposure in Our Environment:** Cut back on the number of unnecessary toxins that are used in personal care and household products. Black women die from cancer at higher rates than any other ethnic group, and environmental toxins are credited with contributing to these high rates of cancer. Go natural whenever you can!

*Please consult your doctor or physician before making any changes to your current diet or exercise routine

In-House Expert! Certified Holistic Health Counselor and Crochet Artist Afya Ibomu

On "Fabulous, Flawless Style from the Inside Out!"

As an Author, Certified Holistic Health Counselor, Entrepreneur, Freelance Journalist and Crochet Artist, Afya Ibomu has built a dynamic reputation in the past 10 years by consistently delivering on her promise to educate, guide and inspire people to live a healthy, natural, and creative lifestyle. www.nattral.com

How can someone interested in transitioning their eating to a more natural regime for a healthy body and hair get started?

I've been a vegetarian for 17 years and a vegan for 10 of those years. It is easy to start by taking one item out of your diet at a time. Choose something you already know that you can easily take out! Remove items one by one every two weeks depending on the point you are at. You can start with pork, chicken, beef, fish or dairy products. Also, you need to add in fruits, vegetables and whole grains, because you want to have balance and make sure you have enough nutrients. Take some things out, but also add some things in!

How does being a vegetarian affect the health of your hair?

In general, people who aren't vegetarians may or may not be aware of their health and the items they eat regularly. Becoming a vegetarian, you become more aware of what you're eating and you read more labels. This starts a cleansing process in your body. A lot of meat and dairy can clog your body and stops your body from taking in the vitamins and minerals as well as it could, which has an effect on your hair. Becoming a vegetarian helps your body to assimilate more nutrients, which benefits your overall health and well-being, including your hair.

For those who may not be ready to leap into vegetarianism, what are the top 5 whole foods that you would recommend incorporating into your diet to promote healthy hair growth?

I like to talk in groups, particularly vitamin A is wonderful for the health of your hair and the way it looks, and you can get vitamin A from red, orange and yellow fruits and vegetables-- tomatoes, red bell peppers and strawberries and carrots are examples. Vitamin C is another vitamin that is wonderful for the health of your hair and you can get that from citrus fruits like oranges and lemons, and leafy greens like collard greens, kale and spinach. Vitamin B is another great vitamin for your hair and can be obtained from brown rice and whole wheat, natural oils – not trans fats or vegetable oils, but fats like nuts and seeds like walnuts, almonds and avocados. Also, water helps your entire body, but also makes your hair less dry and brittle.

What are a few foods that we should avoid?

Definitely avoid trans fats, which are fats that have been changed by heating or a process called hydrogenization, which makes a liquid fat into a solid fat. You can get trans fats from oils like canola oil – they say it's no trans fats, but it's really not a healthy oil for you – margarine and most processed foods, which have trans fats under the name of hydrogenated or partially hydrogenated fats, as well as caffeine, sugar, alcohol, which all take water out of your body and dehydrate you. Avoid white sugar, and white breads daily, which can cause a yeast overgrowth in your body and contribute to dandruff and flaking. Keep it balanced and don't overdo it!

Lasting style really starts internally and flows to the external, and you offer tools for both on your website at nattral.com - what I'm super excited about are your crocheted hats, tell us a little about that!

I have been crocheting for about 11 years, and it started out as a hobby. My mother crocheted when she was pregnant with me, and my family is full of seamstresses and knitters and it came naturally. As soon as I started crocheting hats, they started selling immediately. My hobby turned into a business, and I had my hats at art fairs and boutiques in Brooklyn, NY and over the East Coast. That's where I met Common and have had hats in his video Light, and he introduced me to Erykah Badu, and I made the hat for the cover of her album, Mama's Gun. Crocheting for people as a business and having them in stores, people would want the same style of hat, but just in different colors and sizes. I would never see books in craft stores that represented anything that I would want to wear or what I saw every day in Brooklyn, NY, and that's where the patterns came from. My book Get Your Crochet On! Hip Hats and Cool Caps came out in November of 2006 and so far I've sold 11,000 copies! The names of the hats were influenced by my life and by the names of songs from hip-hop and reggae. I included many illustrations and photos to guide you along.

What are some other creative accessories or ideas that we can use to switch up our look and create fabulous style?

In the book and online, I have a few different designs that can help create styles. One is the Jam Pony, which is a ponytail holder that is a long strip with fringes that come down and creates a very cute way to funk up some ponytails. If you crochet, you can make them any way you want, or you can buy them from my site. Also, I have a bun holder for bad hair days where you still want some flavor, you can put the holder on it, which is fun, cute and they are creative! I also made a crochet head wrap, which you can also make yourself or look at online. It works really well! Head wraps, bun holders and ponytail holders - those are all cute and new and help you to create new and different styles!

6

tools&accessoriesfor**natural**hair**care**

Let's face it! Nappturous divas feel just as strongly about our tools and accessories as Oprah feels about her personal assistants…we can't live without them!

These tools seem to multiply if left unchecked, and have the ability to take over your bathroom…and you thought natural hair would be less maintenance!

The truth is that natural hair IS less maintenance, if you can take the time to determine the systems that work best for your hair, and stick with them.

In line with the best advice I've ever received, develop a relationship with your hair, and it will show you the routine that works best!

To make it easy for you to get started with or tweak your routine, the information in this section will educate and provide easy reference tools for all types of hair and budgets!

What to Use and Where You can Find It

The very best tools that you will use are your own hands and the creativity of your own mind. A tried-and-true method, the "hands on" approach to learning your hair is very effective!

I know a beautiful Nappturous Diva who had a friend do her hair regularly when she transitioned to a natural fro – this was absolutely fine with her until one day, she called to set an appointment and her friend told her "You're going to eventually have to learn how to do this yourself – it's not hard!" She took the cue and began styling her hair herself, and with her hands, creativity, and the right tools, has developed some beautiful and inspiring styles!

Sometimes creative retailers begin creating tools that fall more into the trend category, and have very little functionality. To assess the difference, before you buy an item, ask yourself "Will I be using this item 5 years from now?" If the answer is even slightly hesitant, hold off on shelling out the cash!

Having the right hair tools influences the outcome of styles and the health of the hair. In the book *400 Years Without a Comb*, Willie Lee Morrow elaborates on the detrimental effects on the hair that slaves endured by not having access to the proper grooming tools. This effect was further magnified when tools that were used weren't made to work through the mass of curls and kinks of afro-textured hair. Soon, enterprising African-Americans began manufacturing tools for black hair, and we now live in an age where a multitude of options exist.

We can identify tools that optimize our textures by looking for characteristics that emphasize simplicity, rounded edges, wide teeth, satin finishes, wet heat, and as little friction as possible.

Remember, while others may use tools and proclaim their fabulous results, always look to see that they have a similar hair type or texture as yours before using the same tool looking for a similar result.

While extensive, the following list will be a great start for you, and you can buy new tools as needed. However, I encourage you to obtain the basics first, as noted with an asterisk. Once you obtain everything you need, keep it in its proper place so that you aren't in the bathroom with conditioner running down your back looking for the herb strainer!

Tools of the Fabulous Hair Trade

Hand-held mirror*: You'll be able to more easily examine your scalp, different textures and the consistency of your styles by using a hand-held mirror. Look for one that is shatter proof, as you often will be holding it with slippery hands!

Aquis Microfiber Hair Towel or Turban*: Made of an ultra-lightweight fabric, this super absorbent hair towel will dry your hair quickly without any harsh rubbing necessary! It's great for those with fragile or brittle hair, and using it reduces split ends. The hair turban secures with button enclosure. Gentle treatment is vital for healthy hair care, and this towel gives you added protection. Available at retailers like www.aaaskindoctor.com.

Denman D-3 Brush: The rows of rounded nylon bristles on this brush slide through your conditioner-soaked hair like hot butter, and helps immensely during the detangling process. Only use when your hair is sectioned, wet and has been saturated with conditioner! www.denmanbrush.com

Wide Toothed Comb*: A staple for all curly and kinky headed people! The wide toothed comb should have large, long, plastic teeth that you can use for detangling your hair.

Tail Comb: This comb is used for precise parts and comb twists. I prefer the Mason Pearson brand because each tooth is highly polished to eliminate any rough edges.

100% Boar Bristle Brush*: The boar bristle brush is exclusively used for smoothing styles and for edges, especially at the "kitchen" or nape of the neck!

Soft Toothbrush: For those fly-away curls around the nape and edges of the hair. Just dip in your pomade of choice and brush for a smoother look.

Hair Clips*: Hair clips in various sizes may be one of the most essential tools listed! Use while styling, and to secure hair while retightening or twisting.

Tabletop Hair Dryer: A tabletop hair dryer on low to medium heat can be used to dry your hair or to create an environment of extra conditioning for your hair when combined with a good deep conditioning treatment! Unfortunately, this tool only creates dry heat, and I've found that when conditioning, there is a better option. See the next tool!

Stand Alone Hair Steamer*: Wet heat is preferable to dry heat whenever possible for healthy kinky or curly hair. Another name for wet heat is steam, and steaming combined with a deep conditioner creates a multitude of benefits for tresses that are dry or damaged.

Warm steam helps to open the cuticles of the hair, allowing the restorative ingredients in the deep conditioner to absorb more fully, and quench your mane, adding moisture and strength.

Cheaper Option: Instead of purchasing super-expensive brands from a salon supplier, less expensive alternatives can be found at www.amazon.com, and www.ebay.com.

Even Cheaper Option: Conditioning cap purchased from a beauty supply store and a long steamy shower or sauna at your fitness club!

Cheapest Option: Use a plastic grocery bag!

Bobby Pins and Hair Pins*: For healthy hair, always use hair pins with rounded plastic tips…and once the tip breaks off, trash it! When you pull out a damaged hair pin, it will pull your hair right along with it! Bobby Pins are the closed hair pins that are good for securing hair down in a style. Hair pins are open pins that are a little gentler on your hair.

Hair Bands: Need ponytail holders with grip that won't damage the hair? Scunci created an ingenious brand called No Damage™, that includes satin elastics and head wraps! www.scunci.com

Curlers: Natural hair and locs alike will absolutely love you for using curlers that were made for them! I haven't used a plastic or sponge curler since Diddy was an Intern!

Modern curlers should be made of a softer, pliable material that allows your hair to breathe, creating a faster drying time.

For extremely comfortable curlers that create long-lasting curls, use **Soft Spike Curlers,** which has set the curly gold standard in the loc community! Each set comes in the original and large sizes, and you'll need at least 2 packages for medium thick hair or 3 packages for hair with more length and thickness. www.softspikecurlers.com

Hair Net: Use a hair net not only to secure curlers while air-drying your hair, but if your hair is short, this tool is excellent to use while washing your tresses as a protective measure for the ends of your hair.

Herb Strainers: This is a must have for homemade product junkies! Strain herbs through muslin for a filtered hair tea or clarifying rinse. You can purchase inexpensively online from retailers like:

Muslin drawstring bag for straining herbs: www.thespicehouse.com/spices/muslin-bags

or

3 inch Mesh Tea Ball: www.fromnaturewithlove.com

or

Cheaper Option: Obtain a 5x5 inch piece of muslin from the craft store, spoon herbs into the center and secure with a rubber band! After using, wash the muslin with hand soap and lay out to dry for the next use!

Spray bottles and Containers for Homemade Products: You may want to make more of your favorite product in advance, which is a great time and money saver! Buy new at e-bay or www.fromnaturewithlove.com

Cheaper Option: Reuse old containers and spray bottles if they are made of glass, after sanitizing them thoroughly! Glass containers are the best for re-use.

Satin Scarf or Bonnet*: A satin scarf or bonnet (for styles you don't want flattened) keep your hair in place and protected.

Have trouble keeping the satin scarf on your head at night? Try the ones at www.maverickwear.com, which were specially designed to stay on!

It's best to wash your scarves regularly, and store your scarves and bonnets easily in a special drawer or over-the-door shoe organizer for quick access!

Hair scarves for Locs or long hair*: Often, longer locs fall out of a regular hair scarf, and the ends of the hair that we want to protect are left exposed…and it's not fun to wake up with loc imprints on your cheeks! Two of my favorite options include:

Ayana's Loc Pocket – a head wrap with an ample pocket that you can tuck your long locs into, made of nylon, polyester and spandex. www.glorylocs.com

L.B. Soc – a hair snood made of 100% fine gauge, silky soft polyester. www.denisereed.com

Dreadsock™ – a poly-stretch material used in this hair cover is specially designed for locs. No wraps or ties, it simply slides on for complete comfort and protection. www.dreadsock.com

Satin pillowcase*: Why a satin pillowcase if you're wearing a satin scarf? If you're like me, sometimes my very best effort does not keep the scarf on my head at night! If it happens to fall off, my hair still has a barrier of protection with the satin pillowcase! It is usually easy to find a single satin pillowcase at your local superstore.

Filtered Shower Head: Ever wonder why your hair didn't feel the same after an at-home wash as it did after a salon wash? A little known secret of top salons and stylists is their use of water filters and softeners to produce healthier hair.

Water in our homes is typically classified as "hard water", meaning it contains chemicals, including chlorine and hydrogen sulfide, as well as minerals like calcium and iron, all of which result in hard hair as well!

Use a brand that incorporates an affordable filtration system like the Sprite ShoweRx Filtration System, which balances the ph of water with a durable showerhead. Remember to change the filter on schedule!

Hats: Display your unique personality and preferences while making a fashion statement! Hats make a profound style impact, serve as an extension of your vision of self, and add flavor to your protective styling regime.

Brooklyn-based milliner, Malchijah Hats creates "Your Hats, Your Way" and is known for his "new jack" designs, which are classic in style, yet bespeak originality. www.malchijahhats.net

For all of the boho beauties, Afya Ibomu, the owner of Nattral, has crocheted her way onto the heads of artists Erykah Badu and Common, and has a gorgeous line of crocheted hat options to choose from at www.nattral.com.

Cheaper Option: Afya has written a crochet pattern book release entitled Get Your Crochet On!: Hip Hats and Cool Caps, in which she shares 20 different designs you can crochet yourself!

Head Wraps: African Head Wrapping is an art that defines your individual style and expresses ethnicity in a unique and stylish manner. Artist Erykah Badu breathed life into this ancient tradition when she stepped on the scene, however the craft has been popular for centuries in various cultures.

If you're looking for fashion-forward styles, designer Aishah Bilal creates affordable head wraps, Hijab, Tunics, Turbans, and Sarong skirts. You can even enhance your skills with <u>The Art of Head Wrapping</u> booklet that shows detailed step-by-step instructions for seven different African Head Wrapping methods – break out of the bun! <u>www.bilaldesigns.com</u>

Cheaper Option: Using a 2-yard length of fabric made of nylon or cotton, experiment with different styles.

Tips:

- If you're using a cotton head wrap, first wrap your head with a headscarf to protect your hair.
- If your hats and caps are unlined, take them to your local seamstress and have her add a polyester liner, your hair will thank you!
- For a more extravagant head wrap, use a longer piece of fabric!

Hair Ornaments: Hair ornaments ranging from simple mother-of-pearl hair bands to ornate beaded dangles add spark and assist you in starting your own hair trends!

Not just for loc wearers, Brunsli Hair Ties have experienced rave popularity since being released in 2006! These Nubian-esque art piece hair ties are made from earthy materials like shell, horn, wood and jasper, and can be used to tie your hair back, as a ponytail holder and even as a necklace! Find out more about these crafty hair ties by going to http://hairties.blogspot.com.

The Worst Hair Tools for a Nappturous Diva

Sometimes, there are products on the market that may be for hair, but are not good for **our** natural hair.   Other times, we can take hair tools and their proper usage a little too far! A tool that is usually great for your hair becomes damaging with too much use.

If you see the item on the clearance racks of your local BSS or for a ridiculously cheap price all over e-bay, chances are it may not be the tool you want to grab and run to checkout with!

The following list describes a few of the enemies of Nappturous Divas:

- Small black rubber bands

- Small toothed combs

- Dry heat tools used regularly – flat iron, heating cap, hot comb, hair dryers, etc.

- Hand blow-dryer attachments

- Broken hair pins

- Cotton in bandanas, hair scarves and hats

7

choosinga**natural**hair**salon**

To learn more and get started on the journey towards developing a relationship with your hair, you may need the assistance of a Natural Hair professional. The number Natural Hair salons and Natural Hair Stylists have grown tremendously over the past few years, as more and more women and men have decided to begin embracing their natural texture. From Khamit Kinks in Brooklyn, NY to Mandisa Ngozi in Tallahassee, FL, textured hair folk can relax their hair and spirits in an uplifting atmosphere, sip herbal teas and receive treatments that proclaim and enhance the glory of their locks.

On the flip side, there are those salons who are simply trying to get "in on the trend," who say they offer natural services, but may not have had the experience or training. This informative section will help you determine the difference between the two, and equip you with easy ways to develop a great relationship with a stylist. You have the power! The consumer's demands shape the market, as we can see with the multitude of hair products now available that did not exist five years ago. As we share more of our preferences with those who want to provide quality services, the more the industry will shape to fit our needs.

Why every Cosmetologist may not possess the experience of a Natural Hair stylist, and why some Natural Hair Stylists may not be Cosmetologists

In most states, a cosmetology student is required to take 1,600 hours of training at a cosmetology school, and pay for a curriculum that does not cover any of the aspects of braiding and caring for natural hair, a craft that is hundreds of years old. The expense of cosmetology school can be up to $10,000 in major metropolitan cities or as low as $6,500 in rural areas, and the average school may not offer financial aid. For a stylist who has gained experience outside of a cosmetology setting, investing the time and money to gain a certificate that validates what they were already doing is viewed as a major inconvenience. These requirements lead to the inevitable – stylists who do hair in the home, risking jail time and fines exceeding $1,000!

A remarkable example is that of Isis, a Natural Hair Stylist in Dallas, Texas, who was charged with breaking cosmetology regulations and illegally braiding hair without a license. Although she was found guilty, there was no violation at that time that the state was able to create, so Isis continued offering services to her loyal clientele. In 1997, state officials barged into her salon, handcuffed and arrested her, and she fought back, eventually working the braiding requirement down from 1,600 to only 35 hours of useful information.

Some states, under pressure from proactive local braiders and Natural Hair Stylists who submitted legislation demanding fair treatment, have revised their approach to categorizing our ancient craft of braiding and locking as cosmetology. These states include New York, California, Texas and some others which have determined that a full cosmetology license is no longer necessary for a Natural Hair Stylist, or have developed a braider's certificate program which teaches topics including scalp care and sanitation over a 20-40 hour curriculum.

This means that the most useful factors for you to consider when selecting a Natural Hair Stylist may not be printed on a license. The top aspects to consider when selecting a stylist are:

1. **Experience** – An experienced Natural Hair Stylist should have a portfolio of clients that they have personally styled. If you have a particular hair concern, determine if this stylist suits you by looking at pictures of clients with similar issues. If a picture is not available, ask the stylist for a client referral and call them personally!

2. **Disposition** – Look for a stylist with a great chair-side manner, similar to a doctor's bedside manner! Give extra bonuses for a stylist who has natural hair or locs, because they have gone through the transitions that you will be going through, and should be able to counsel and provide advice for both your physical and emotional questions and concerns. You should feel positive and empowered about your hair once they are done providing your service.

3. **Technique** – An informed stylist will always ask to touch and examine your hair during an initial consultation or at the beginning of your appointment. They should also ask you questions about your hair history and help to shape expectations and share their treatment process with you. Ask about the ingredients in the products they are using. Their philosophy should be in line with your ideals. Don't compromise what you want simply because you are in a salon! Look for an open, hands-on approach from your stylist, and

take your products with you to the salon if you have a great stylist, but don't care for the products or ingredients that are used.

Interviewing Your Potential Stylist

Increasing evidence confirms that new standards are being set among Natural Hair Stylists. I recently was informed about a Natural Hair Stylist who not only performs a detailed analysis of your hair during a consultation, but also prints out a set of personalized hair instructions at the end of the consultation. At the first hair appointment, she provides a Product Consultation, and asks you to bring all of your products with you in a basket. She then goes through each of the products and lets you know which ones to continue using! The level of quality and informed service are changing in the natural hair community, and the stylists who are at the forefront are recognizing this shift and adjusting accordingly.

Some stylists may have the experience, but are not as savvy as the stylist detailed above. If you locate a stylist like this who you would like to visit, politely set up an in-person consultation (preferred) or telephone conversation with your potential stylist so that you can conduct an interview of your own. With a good nature, ask questions including:

1. How long have you been doing natural hair or locs?

2. Have you studied under a Master Natural Hair Artist or Loctician?

3. May I see your portfolio?

4. What ingredients are in the products you use?

5. How do you feel about me bringing my own products?

6. What technique will you use to get my hair from point A to point B?

7. What is your late or no-show policy?

8. Is it possible for me to reach you on a cell number?

9. When is the best time during the day for me to schedule an appointment with you?

10. How do you counsel your clients through transitions?

Back In the Day…

When I moved to the Midwest in the late 90's, I decided to trek out one day in search of a natural hair salon. I was working in a new city, and needed a style that I could wear professionally with flexibility. I am from the South, where options for natural hair salons were more plenteous, and I thought for sure I would find someone who would be able to do my hair. Talk about a total culture shock! Every stylist I met that day either suggested that I get a relaxer or a weave, and the braiding shops wouldn't even braid my hair without extensions! By the end of the day I was tired of explaining that no, I didn't want a relaxer, no, you cannot hot comb my hair and no, extensions were not what I was interested in! In search of a great style at a Natural Hair salon, I flew to New York and set an appointment at Tendrils in Brooklyn. My spirit was opened to what was possible! The at-home feeling of the salon, vibrant affirmation of my hair in its kinky, voluminous, natural state and the end result of time well-spent were evidence that a culture existed where I would have support for my choice…except that it was about 1,500 miles away!! My solution at that time was to bring that essence to the Midwest and open a Natural Hair Salon, which I did less than a year later.

Fortunately, there are more options for Nappturous Divas today, and a good Natural Hair Stylist is just a short referral away!

Nappturous Diva's Principle #2

We Appreciate Our Texture

We know that every texture has its Celebrations as well as its Challenges. We are continually discovering and appreciating the uniqueness of our God-given curls and coils, and styling it in ways that complement our texture.

No two heads of hair are the same. Some will have a wavier texture, and some a more coiled texture. Some have fragile hair, while others have hair that possesses a more durable nature. It is a beautiful place to be when you make peace with your tresses and capitalize on its strengths, while learning to accept others and the hair they have been blessed with. Our goal is to continually improve what we have been given, and when we cease comparisons and enjoy the blessing of our texture, we are able to see more options, have more patience and give our hair permission to just BE…and it will flourish in thanks to you! Once we give all of our sisters, whether relaxed or natural, the room to love what they have, no one assuming a superior position, we will shine in the glory of healthy self-love and acceptance reflecting from our inner beings. Within Nappturous Diva Principle #2, we will locate your specific hair texture, helping you to make more accurate product selections, define the volume of your hair, debunk myths about natural hair and locs, and explore the world of locs as a styling option for optimizing textured hair!

findingyour**hair**texture

Begin by selecting a single strand of the most common type of hair on your head, particularly if you have several different hair textures. The hair should be product-free and dry.

If you are transitioning, refer to at least 2 inches of natural hair only, from the scalp to the point of transition. Take the strand and pull it tight, and then let it go. Did it:

a. Fall   right   back   down   into   loose   coils   in   a   spiraling   S   shape?

b. Fall down with a slight spring, and a spiraling S shape?

c. Spring back slightly into a medium-tight corkscrew, in an O or S shape?

d. Spring back half of the way with a tight O-shaped coil?

e. Spring back up completely with a Z-shaped coil?

If you answered:

A – You have 3A hair, which is very loosely curled and usually very shiny with larger ringlets. The bends in your hair occur infrequently, about every 1-inch. The shorter the hair is, the straighter it gets. The longer the hair is, the more apparent the curl. You have shiny, smooth curls, which are prone to frizz when introduced to humidity.

B – You have 3B hair, which has a medium amount of curl with a diameter of about ½ inch. When wet, it appears to be fairly wavy, but as it dries, absorbs the water and shrinks. Your curls are shiny, well defined and springy.

C – You have 3C hair, which looks like a multitude of small corkscrews, or curls in a cylindrical O wave pattern. The curls have a diameter of about ¼ inch, and can be either kinky, or very tightly curled, with many densely packed strands.

D – You have 4A hair, which is defined by kinky, tight coils that, when stretched, have a very tight O pattern. 4A hair has a cottony texture, is fragile, and also may appear coarse, but when healthy, is soft to the touch.

E – You have 4B hair, which has a very kinky, tightly zigzagged Z pattern, and less of a defined curl pattern. Instead of curling or coiling, the hair has many frequent bends in sharp angles like the letter Z. 4B hair also has a wiry texture, is fragile, doesn't retain much moisture, and appears coarse but is soft to the touch.

It is very common for one person to possess several different textures of hair. Usually, the patch of hair that will have the curliest texture is in the crown of the head.

Knowledge of what texture your hair is helps you to know how to handle your hair and what types of product combinations work best for you. More coiled, textured hair is more fragile than wavier hair, and needs more frequent moisturizing. Wavier hair is more commonly longer in its natural state, and requires more patience when detangling. You'll learn more about how to handle your hair as we continue this journey together.

determiningthevolumeofyourhair

Think about the difference between hair that has been relaxed and the same head of hair that is natural. The difference in the volume of the hair is amazing…especially for those who thought they had thin hair!! If you are a survivor of relaxers, a.k.a. "chemical fire creams", the natural glory you now possess probably extends beyond a thickness you never imagined!

The volume of your hair depends on a number of variables, including diameter, density, stiffness, and curvature.

Diameter refers to the size of each hair strand, and is usually most affected by a healthy and nutritious eating plan. Products sometimes temporarily enhance the diameter of the hair by coating them with polymers and glossy substances, or with large molecules that cannot penetrate the hair cuticle, as in the case of semi-permanent hair color. This creates a temporary outcome of thicker looking hair.

Density is the number of hairs that you have per square centimeter, typically between 160 and 300, if you are an adult. Teenagers often seem to have thick hair, and that is because hair density peaks around 16 years of age and decreases as we get older.

Hair stiffness refers to how far your hair lies away from the scalp, and is directly related to thickness.

The curvature of your hair is described by the number of bends each strand of hair has. More curves increase the amount of space the hair takes up, causing the hair to consume more room.

The smoother the cuticle and the fewer curves in the hair, the shiner it appears. The rougher the cuticle and the more curves, the less shiny the hair appears.

Afro-textured hair tends to have more curves and bends than straight hair textures; therefore, it reflects less light and appears less shiny. If you have a 3C, 4A or 4B texture, instead of shiny hair, make it a goal to have smooth, healthy cuticles that increase the sheen of the hair. Products like apple cider vinegar increase the sheen of the hair due to the acidic content, which assists the hair cuticle in lying down.

What is Your Hair Volume?

Those with thick hair volume have hair that is very dense. You cannot see through the hair or see the scalp without parting and separating the hair. Medium hair volume is less dense, and you may be able to see through some sections of the hair. Fine hair volume describes hair with a fewer number of total hairs, and you can easily see through the hair to the scalp.

One of my Nappturous Diva friends, Michelle* is a savvy Real Estate Investor and Counselor who loves to help couples repair their marriages and, in her free time, enjoys dances around the living room with her three year old daughter. She always kept her hair relaxed and very stylish, but even with long 3-month braid breaks, she couldn't repair an area of her hair that continually broke off. Not just that, but she always felt her hair was on the thinner side. After years of dealing with this and still having the problem, she loc'd her hair. After only 6 months, she shared with me that not only was that damaged section of her hair completely repaired; she couldn't even describe her hair as "on the thinner side" anymore. Her natural locs have a volume and sheen that she feels great about and consistently gets compliments on. *Not her real name

Many Nappturous Divas with fine hair have noted that having natural hair has been a wonderful experience for them because their hair feels and appears much thicker than when they had relaxers. The more curls and kinks, the more volume the hair appears to have! Even on a bad hair day, natural hair is all good!

findingyour**hair**care**regime**

Now that you know your hair type and volume, one of the easiest ways to determine what routine your hair needs is by using the **Nappturous Diva's Hair Care Routine Easy Reference Guide.** Use this guide as a general place to start, and as you learn more about your hair, be free to experiment and add your own knowledge.

Nappturous Divas Hair Care Regime Easy Reference Guide

To assist you in maximizing the use of this guide, ask yourself the following questions, and then match your hair texture and hair challenges with the routines with the guide below:

1. Is your hair colored?
2. Do you have dandruff or scalp issues?

3. Are you concerned about length?

4. Are you transitioning from a relaxer?

5. Would you like to add more moisture?

6. How much time would you like to set aside for your hair routine?

7. What day is conducive to your schedule?

8. Are you going to include a stylist or salon in your routine, or are you going to be the sole stylist for your hair?

9. Is your hair newly loc'd?

10. Are you following any strict rules for your hair care, as with new locs?

11. Are you on medication that affects your hair?

12. Do you have a medical condition such as high blood pressure that affects the types of ingredients you can safely use?

All of these questions affect your hair care routine and need to be answered so that you can begin to craft the system that works best for you, and for all of the other "natural heads" you may be responsible for!

Nappturous Divas Hair Care Regime - Easy Reference Guide

Hair Type

3A: Pre-Poo EW, Shampoo Set WN, Poo EW, Condition EW, Deep Condition OM, Clarify OM, Detangle EW, Moisturize WN

3B: Pre-Poo EW, Shampoo Set WN, Poo EW, Condition EW, Deep Condition OM, Clarify OM, Detangle EW, Moisturize WN

3C: Pre-Poo EW, Shampoo Set WN, Poo EW, Condition EW, Deep Condition TM, Clarify OM, Detangle EW, Moisturize WN

4A: Pre-Poo EW, Shampoo Set WN, Poo EW, Deep Condition EW, Clarify TM, Detangle EW, Moisturize Daily or WN

4B: Pre-Poo EW, Shampoo Set WN, Poo EW, Deep Condition EW, Clarify TM, Detangle EW, Moisturize Daily or WN

For the Following Special Conditions, add on:

Dry Scalp/Dandruff: Deep condition EW, Clarify EW until clear

Color: Deep condition EW

Transitioning: Detangle EW, Condition EW, Clarify EW/WC, Moisturize Daily

Maintain Length: Detangle EW, Condition EW, Deep condition TM, Clarify EW/WC, Moisturize Daily

Dry Hair: Pre-Poo EW, Deep Condition EW, Clarify EW/WC, Moisturize Daily

EW = Every Wash, OM = Once a Month, TM = Twice a Month, WN = When Needed, WC = With Care

hairmyths**and**the**truth**revealed**!**

Myth #1: A little grease on the scalp helps to moisturize.

Although we may have grown up using grease, the primary ingredients in most grease products are petrolatum and mineral oil, which do not absorb easily into the skin. These ingredients also dry the hair out and impede hair growth by clogging the pores.

Myth #2: The same hair products that worked then, work now.

Sometimes true, but I would recommend checking the label because products change. There are newer products made specifically for natural hair or loc that work more effectively and can help you achieve the results you want.

Myth #3: Kinky, coiled hair doesn't grow!

The truth is that all hair grows. The speed upon which your hair grows depends on a variety of factors ranging from hair type and nutrition, to hereditary and environmental variables.

Many times, people with curlier hair textures do not see the growth because of hair breakage. Each bend in the hair is a potential breaking point. The more bends, the more breaking points. The growth is still happening, but the ends of the hair are being broken off more frequently, making it appear as though the hair is not growing. To see hair growth, you should increase the length of time your hair spends in protective styles, which shield the ends of your hair from the environment, and consider increasing your moisture routine.

Myth #4: Water dries my hair out!

Did you know that water makes up ¼ of the weight of a strand of hair? Just like the rest of your body, your hair needs water both internally and externally to remain supple! If you're thirsty, you have already lost too much water; so imagine what is happening to dry hair! Replenish the water your hair needs on a daily basis with a homemade spritz of water and essential oils.

Myth #5: Reading ingredient labels is too hard; there are too many different ingredients to remember.

Although there are more ingredients in most products than hair salons on MLK, Jr. Drive in your city, the more you read the labels, the more you'll recognize the harmful ingredients.

A key to remember is that ingredients that you can pronounce and are familiar to you are typically the ingredients that are safe.

To go the easy route, look for products that advertise the use of natural oils, essential oils, or high-quality ingredients and even then, check the label!

Myth #6: I don't have to wrap my hair in a satin scarf because it's natural now, or because I've had natural hair for a while and it's too long.

Do you care about moisture? Lint? Your skin? Length?

Sure you do! Then refuse to let that cotton pillowcase absorb the moisture right out of your hair! Keeping your hair wrapped or appropriately hooded with a satin scarf or bonnet ensures not only that your hair's moisture is retained, but it also keeps lint out (a problem that more and more natural hair and loc wearers are experiencing), protects the ends of your hair from friction-causing tossing and turning, and keeps the products on your hair from interacting with the skin, which can cause breakouts!

Myth #7: Trimming my hair is not necessary now that I'm natural!

It may sound like an oxymoron, but regularly trimming the hair by small amounts can actually help your hair to grow longer!

Damage done to the ends of the hair begins inside the hair strand, and splits internally, up the hair shaft. If left unchecked, this damage will cause you to need a major haircut! Our hair grows at a rate of ½ inch per month, so if you trim ¼ inch every eight weeks, by the end of the year, you will have a cumulative growth of three healthy inches, versus having to cut off five or six inches of split ends. Additionally, your hair will be less coarse and tangled on the ends, making it easier to comb and style.

locoptions**for**textured**hair**

Textured hair is glorious when worn a variety of different ways, and women with afro-textured hair are beautiful in loose, twisted, braided, and loc'd styles. Here, we will explore the loc'd experience. If you've ever been curious about locs-- whether you've considered starting them or currently wear them, this section explains everything that you need to know!

The Loc'd Experience

Locs

Locs have their origin in the African Diaspora, but various cultures, from the Naga Indians to the ancient Greeks, wore locs for different reasons. Tribal communities in Africa, including the Pokot,

Massai, Mau Mau, Kau, Ashanti and Fulani, have worn locs in a variety of unique manners. Rastafarian wearers of locs call them "dreadlocks", and believe them to be a physical way of rejecting Babylon and its influences. This ancient tradition is yet another example of the diversity in natural hair.

The Mental Process

The transition of your hair to locs requires a mental shift. You must prepare your mind, your space, your tools and how you will handle those around you as you loc your hair, similarly to how you changed your environment – both mentally and physically – when you first transitioned to natural hair. Developing your Natural Hair Manifesto for locs is just as important and can help you to solidify a healthy mental foundation as your hair changes!

You will have days where you love your hair, and some people who have locs enjoy the entire process. However, the majority of people will have days where they look in the mirror and wonder what possessed them to ever consider locing their hair. These fluctuations in feeling will pass, and as your locs mature, your ability to adjust to the transition will mature as well.

The Stages of Locing

Many locticians have described between three and six different stages that you will experience when making the transition to locs. I have chosen four primary stages, each with its own set of challenges and celebrations!

Stage One: Baby Locs

After choosing your method to start locing, you or your stylist will start you on your way. If you've chosen a cultivated loc option, you may recognize the style of coils, two-strand twists or braids that are installed as a style you've worn before. Your hair will become fuzzier as the days go by, and the longer coils, braids and twists will most likely shrink in length. Typical 3c, 4a and 4b hair will remain in this stage for three to six months. If your hair is 3a or 3b in texture, it may take longer for you to begin seeing the key indicator, budding, and know that you have moved on to the next stage.

Stage Two: Teenage Locs

Budding occurs when the loc begins to form firm, rounded, matted sections of hair appearing along the length of the loc, typically in the middle or towards the end. Your locs will also become increasingly fuzzy and larger in appearance, and despite styling attempts, will sometimes seem to have a mind of their own! This stage can begin to occur as early as three months, but may take up to 18 months, depending on your hair texture.

Stage Three: Adult Locs

The Stage Three usually lasts between one to two years. Locs that reach the Adult stage begin to smooth down and compact. You will recognize this stage when your locs appear smaller than they were in Stage Two, and more uniform in size. The loc will have developed from the bud, and then out in both directions towards the scalp and end of the loc. During this stage you will also notice what will seem like extraordinary growth! Although your hair has been growing at the same rate, the weight of the loc will begin to pull the hair downward, making growth more noticeable.

Stage Four: Mature Locs

Locs can become Mature in as soon as 18 months or as long as 3 years. At this point, the locs have formed a complex, tightly interwoven matrix of hair throughout the length of the loc, and are solid and uniform in appearance. Mature locs are strong, and if maintained well, very easy to style.

How You Know When You are Loc'd

The process of locing occurs in different timeframes, depending on your hair texture. When I was initially Sisterlocked, it was the first time I was told that I had "good hair!" Good hair for locing, that is. Although all healthy hair is "good hair", 4a and 4b hair types will loc faster than hair with a looser texture. All hair types, however, can loc depending on the level of cultivation and care the wearer is willing to maintain! As you transition through the four stages that all loc wearers must go through, whether freeform, traditional, Sisterlocks™, Nappylocs or Bradelocz, once your hair is left uncombed, it will begin to coil upon itself and create locs. Three easy ways to know if you are loc'd:

1. The buds in your locs are no longer distinguishable from the rest of your loc
2. Hair that was once "fuzzy" begins to lay down within the loc
3. If cultivated, your hair has lost the "patterned" appearance of the method that was used to begin them, and have a smooth, round shape

In-House Expert! Master Loctician Thierry Baptiste

On "Locs Equal Freedom"

Thierry Baptiste possesses such a rare and unique approach to locs that once introduced to his style, clients have been known to be absolutely addicted! Thierry's secret to success is that he is never complacent to what's going on in the industry and is constantly creating new standards for our hair in locs. His current vice is hair color and his applications are sure to be the foundation of color techniques for natural hair in the future. He encourages his clients both to embrace their HAIRITAGE and dream! www.thierrybaptiste.com

What are the top 3 reasons that your clients decide to transition to locs?

First, spiritually, this is how our hair is supposed to be. You can go back to the tombs of Nefertiti, you can take it back to the beginning of time and the original man, and you would see artifacts of our people wearing locs. This is what comes naturally. Second, economically, due to the state of our world today, we are at a financial drought and do not have the means to be in the beauty shop every week! Wearing our hair naturally and wearing locs, we are able to go to the salons with less visits, save money and still look great! Women with locs look better on their way back into the salon than they do when they leave. Locs are the only hairstyle that you get more compliments on as the days progress. Third, the infinite possibilities of hairstyles you can do with locs last much longer! A roller set on locs will last twice the time that a roller set on straight hair will last. Locs are just longer strands of hair. We as a people realize that locs are another way to express the concept of being natural and being chic.

For our readers who may not know, what is the difference between a Natural Hair Stylist and a Loctician?

I began as a Natural Hair Stylist and did a variation of natural hairstyles, which can consist of anything from styling afros to twists to two-strands to locs, or any hairstyle where someone did not have their hair chemically treated. Being a Loctician I am specializing my services in locs only. If you had a heart attack and had to go to the hospital, would you go to a general practitioner, or a heart specialist? We need our hair! If you love your locs are you going to go to a natural hair specialist or a Loctician?

You've developed a reputation that has transcended "Loctician"– and are one of the pioneers in the fashion of locs in that you've done everything from writing editorial articles for natural hair magazines, to runway hair design– what are some of your secret "insider" styling tips?

One of the simplest things that consumers can do in reference to styling their hair is working in sections. We have so much hair on our heads and trying to style an entire cascade of locs can be overwhelming. Whatever style you are doing, part your hair into six sections and work on one section at a time, being repetitive with what you do in each section and it will all come out complete.

What is your opinion on how locs equal freedom for so many people?

I believe the most important thing learned when one obtains locs is patience. Locs are not an overnight hairstyle! You cannot leave a Loctician and have locs on day one. Locs normally take 2-3 months to start maturing for each person. When you learn patience you can redirect that energy into other areas of our lives. Economically we are victims of ADD. We want it instantly and we want everything overnight. When we learn to appreciate the fact that our hair was something that we nurtured and watered and flowered and later see it blossom we can redirect that energy into other areas of our lives and as a people grow.

Describe the condition your hair should be in for a Loctician to start a healthy head of locs?

First, you need to be in a positive state of mind. State of mind is very, very important. You have to be positive! I tell clients to expect the unexpected! I have no magic wand to tell you how your hair is going to turn out. Everyone has different DNA. Your hair has to be healthy, and your ends need to be trimmed. Your state of mind, intake of water, and your physical health are all very important. It's much deeper than the condition of the strands of hair; it is your whole essence that is important to the foundation of your locs. There are so many people who don't like the beginning stages of their locs. They want shoulder length locs and won't be happy until their hair gets to their shoulders. So anything until that is not satisfying to them. With that state of mind, your hair will never get to your shoulders! You have to embrace every stage of development.

How have your loc'd clients successfully melded their hairstyle with a Corporate environment?

Our hair is regal. There is nothing closer to royalty than our African descent hair. As African Americans we need to know our rights! We cannot let anyone in Corporate America tell us that we cannot wear our hair in its natural state. If someone tells you that, have them put it on company letterhead and you own that company! That is illegal for someone to tell you that you cannot wear your hair natural in Corporate America...it's ILLEGAL! It really is much deeper than Corporate America; it's in our churches and social groups. We have to redefine our standards of beauty and incorporate natural hair and locs into our definition of beauty. The problem is that we've gone our entire lives thinking that this one look is beautiful and then we're exposed to ourselves, and we say, "OK, I've gone my whole life looking this way and I'm too old to change!" We do not have to change as a people, just incorporate that! Just expand. Our locs are an expression of our freedom!

I know how you are always in what I call "creation mode", what do you have on the horizon that we should be on the lookout for?

What I am doing now is creating a lifestyle where I'm trying to get our people to embrace life. The key word that I am going to use today with you for the first time, and I'm going to take this word and manifest it throughout the world is Acceptance. We have to learn to accept who we are. We have to learn to accept that someone might

110

not like it! Accept the fact that this is your texture. Your hair may be nappy, and it's beautiful. Your hair may be wavy and it's beautiful. What are we saying to our young people – that we need 3 bags of horsehair to be beautiful? We need to pay more respect to elders and look to them for guidance. Acceptance is the foundation of my journey.

The Methods Used to Start Locs

There are different methods used to start locs, including freeforming, as well as cultivated loc options, like coils, two-strand twists, braids, Braidlocs and the patented processes, Nappylocs and Sisterlocks™. For every method, excluding Sisterlocks™, you will need at least two-three inches of natural hair, and all relaxed ends must be trimmed completely.   There are also different methods used to maintain the new growth that occurs at the root, including twisting and palm rolling, and types of latching, which I will discuss in this section.

Things to Consider as You Are Starting Your locs

A few questions need to be considered as you think about starting your locs. Do you want small, medium or large locs? Do you want uniform parting? Do you want your locs to be symmetrical? You can pull your hair apart at the base and begin your locs if you aren't concerned about uniform parting, but if you prefer a symmetrical sizing for your locs, it may be easier to part your hair as you go. The parting of your locs will determine the ultimate size of your locs. Usually, a part the size of 1/4 of an inch at the base of a coil will form into the size of a thin pencil.

Freeforming

One of the simplest ways to start locs is through freeforming. This method requires only that you wash your hair normally and apply moisturizers as necessary. As you begin to see sections matting, separate the sections from each other by pulling gently. Some freeformed or organic loc wearers believe that pulling and oil are not required. Simply continue washing your hair, and the natural coiling process will begin to happen, because the essence of the creation of freeform locs is to refrain from cultivation like twisting the root-beds. By six months, you will see the coils begin to mesh and matt upon themselves, and the hair will begin to loc. By twelve months, you should have solid budding throughout the middle to the ends of the locs. The locs will naturally assume a cylindrical shape, and become different sizes and lengths.

Pros

- Low Maintenance, organically grown hair
- You can wash and rinse your hair as often as you like!

Finger Rolling

In the finger rolling method, the loc is formed by separating the slightly damp hair at the root with the index finger and thumb, rolling it clockwise into a coil, and securing each loc with a hairclip until dry. A small amount of pure Aloe Vera gel and jojoba or other lightweight oil should be applied to the sections of hair being finger rolled to help it maintain its shape. Waxes and heavy butters are not necessary, and will only build-up in the loc, becoming very difficult, if not impossible, to remove.

The coils can be small or large in diameter, depending upon the final size desired by the wearer. Care should be taken not to part the coils any smaller than the size of ¼ of an inch, because as the locs grow longer, the weight of the loc will put stress on the root-bed, and if the root-bed is too thin, the locs will break off. Additionally, twisting the locs too often will also apply inordinate amounts of stress to the root-bed, causing breakage, so keep the time between retwisting sessions to a minimum of four weeks.

Pros

- Size of the loc can be controlled, if desired
- Easy to maintain yourself

Comb Coils or Two-strand twists

The most popular method used to start locs is through comb coiling or two-strand twisting. Using these methods, the hair is parted with the tail end of the comb into small squares and then coiled into a cylindrical shape with the tooth-end of the comb, or divided in two and twisted around solidly. As in the finger rolling method, a light coating of Aloe Vera gel and oil will help the coil or twist maintain its cylindrical shape without causing build up. If started with a two-strand twist, the pattern of the twist will mesh and become a solid loc after approximately six months.

Pros

- Size of the loc can be controlled, if desired
- Easy to maintain yourself

Braidlocs

Braidlocs, also known as Bradelocz, can go by many names but are defined as locs that are started with braids. This concept originated with those who wanted to start locs and be able to immediately style or wash them without the maintenance concerns of traditional cultivated locs. This method, although not the same as Sisterlocks™ or Nappylocs, is also promoted by those who prefer an inexpensive alternative that they can personally start and maintain.

Things to Know About Braidlocs:

- As your Braidlocs mature, the pattern of the braid will smooth out and your locs will take on a smooth, solid cylindrical shape
- Braid your hair securely, but not too tightly, as this is not necessary
- Natural manipulation is fine for Braidlocs, and will not slow the locing process
- All relaxed ends need to be completely trimmed for effective Braidlocing
- Stay away from styling with hot tools and opt instead for the texture gained from twisting and braiding your Braidlocs
- To maintain the new growth that has occurred since you installed Braidlocs, use the twisting or Latching method, described in detail below

Pros

- Smaller size lends to increased versatility and styling options
- Can be washed with care immediately – no waiting
- Very inexpensive to install
- You can start Braidlocs yourself!

Instructions for Starting Your Own Braidlocs or Traditional Locs with Coils or Two-Strand Twists

1. Part your hair vertically, from the front of your hairline to the nape of your neck, and then part it again horizontally from the top of one ear to the top of the other. Your hair is now

divided into four equal sections. A vertical part is important if you will want to wear styles with your locs that require a center part.

2. Clip all sections down except the back left section.

3. Part your hair horizontally at the nape of your neck for your first row.

4. Vertically part to form a square and begin braiding/coiling/two-strand twisting each section.

5. The square parting you make will determine the ultimate size of your locs. Remember, it is the size of the part, not the size of the braid/coil/two-strand twist that will form the resulting size of your loc! Your braids/coils/two-strand twists will be smaller when you are newly loc'd but will expand as the locing process continues. They will follow the same locing transitions that traditional locs follow, and compact down once they are mature.

6. After braiding/coiling/two-strand twisting one section, clip it to the side, and go to the back right section.

7. Continue to part using the previous section as a guide, and braid/coil/two-strand twist that section. You can also count the locs on either side of the center part to ensure symmetry.

8. Finish off the two front sections, being careful to part as you go, and you're done!

Nappylocs

The Nappylocs system locs hair using a locing tool that comes in varying sizes for very small locs, to large locks. The tool is worked similarly to the latching method described later on, but much of the appeal of this system is that for less than $100, you can order the complete *Making Dreadlocks Using a Tool* book, video and a small, medium or large tool to do the system yourself at home. The Nappylocs method is also good for maintaining locks that have been created using any other system. Using any type of tool decreases the tension on the root-bed and ensures little to no slippage after a loc maintenance session.

Pros

- You can create very small to large locs using the Nappylocs tool
- Can be washed with care immediately – no waiting
- Self-Installation kit is affordable. Available at www.nappylocs.com

Sisterlocks™

Who knew that when Dr. Joanne Cornwell created Sisterlocks™ in 1993, so many people would experience radical "hair emancipation!" Since then, hundreds of women and men have enjoyed the freedom of their Sisterlocks™ and Brotherlocks™, respectively. Sisterlocks™ are a type of cultivated loc that is performed with a patented method. They are small compared to most traditional locs, and their smaller size adds flexibility in styling and a non-traditional look that is unique and appealing to the wearers.

Every person who wants Sisterlocks™ is guided through the Sisterlocks™ process by a <u>Certified Sisterlocks Consultant</u> (CSC), and goes through 3 visits to their CSC to complete the initial locking system. You cannot install Sisterlocks™ personally, unless you are a Certified Sisterlocks Consultant.

Getting Your Sisterlocks

Step one is the Sisterlocks™ Consultation, where a CSC will examine and install a few test locks that you'll wear for about two shampoos, as well as answer your questions.

During step two, you'll have your Sisterlocks™ locing session, the length of which depends on various factors like the length of the natural hair that will be loc'd, the thickness of your hair and the speed of your CSC.

The last step is the Retightening session, where your CSC will repair any slippage and add any new growth into to the locs.

As always, I recommend going into your Consultation as informed as possible. A few ways to gather information about Sisterlocks™ are:

1.	Read the official Sisterlocks™ site, at www.sisterlocks.com. This site is locked and loaded with information about the Sisterlocks™ process, including FAQ's, a beautiful photo gallery and the Official Certified Sisterlock™ Consultant Registry, so that you can find a recommended CSC near you. Always check credentials!

2.   Join the LockItUp Yahoo group. If you have a Yahoo account, simply go to LockItUp-subscribe@yahoogroups.com to join!

3.   View pictures of Sisterlocks™. First remember to take note of your texture and find pictures of others who have a similar texture and thickness, before saying "I want my hair to look like that!" Print out the photos you like to take to the consultation with your CSC.

Pros

- Smaller locs maintained with the Sisterlocks™ method are stronger than the same sized locs maintained by twisting and palm rolling
- Relaxed ends do not need to be trimmed off to start Sisterlocks
- Can be washed with care immediately – no waiting
- Certified Sisterlock™ Consultant registry allows increased confidence when getting your Sisterlocks™ because you know that the CSC has been approved by the Sisterlock™ home office
- Retightening class offered after 6 months allows you to retighten your own hair, saving money! You will be supplied the tool necessary to retighten, and it should be included in

the fee for the class. Retightening your hair can be done over the course of a few days, a little at a time, so it's easy to fit it into your schedule.

Caring for your Locs

Caring for your locs is easy and simple. Use the same product regimes prescribed for traditional loc wearers and refrain from creamy or shea butter based products, as these will clog your hair follicles and build-up in your locs, slowing locing progression and causing styles to have weak staying power. As your locs mature, wash your hair according to the steps described in the Basic Maintenance section of this book. If your locs are new and were started with the finger rolling, comb coil or two-strand twist methods, you should wait four to six weeks for your locs to set before washing. If you have a 3a or 3b texture that is made of looser, sleeker curls, take extra precaution while washing your hair by incorporating the Shampoo Set described in Chapter Four until you are comfortable that your locs are forming and not slipping when wet. For additional assistance, see the next section on **Nappturous Diva's Top 5 Mistakes Sisterlock™ Wearers Make.** These same concepts apply to Braidlocs, Nappylocs and small cultivated loc wearers as well.

13

mistakestoavoid
for Sisterlock™, Nappylocs and Braidlocs Wearers

To have the best experience with your locs, be aware of **Nappturous Diva's Solutions for the Top Five Mistakes Newbie and Mature Sisterlock™, Nappylocs and Braidlocs Wearers Make.** ***These solutions also apply to any other type of small cultivated loc***:

Nappturous Diva's Solutions for the Top Five Mistakes Newbie Sisterlock™ Wearers Make:

1. **Not Bundling your locs before washing.** Although this step is specific to Sisterlocks™ wearers, all new locs should be bundled, or

2. braided and banded before they hit water, and separated at the base afterwards to prevent the locs from meshing and growing together! The length of time spent in this stage depends on how long it takes for your locs to mature to the point where bunching

121

and slippage are no longer a concern. For some hair textures, such as 4A or 4B, slippage may not be a concern at all, but bundling and separating is still recommended.

3. **Continuing with the same product routine you had before Sisterlocks™, Nappylocs or Braidlocs.** The recommendation given by locticians to discontinue the product junkie habit is founded in a reason! Because of the smaller nature of these types of locs, products, particularly those that were fine for your hair before locing, can get trapped within your newly forming locs and you will see the results of product build-up later on in your locing process. Your locs will not hold styles as well and curls will fall easily because of the amount of product trapped in the loc. For beautiful, well-moisturized locs, use lightweight products or products that are specially formulated for your type of locs, particularly in the beginning. Ensure that any products outside of this routine do not cause build-up and are made with oils that are close to the natural sebum in our skin, like jojoba oil.

4. **Coloring too soon after getting Sisterlocks™, Nappylocs and Braidlocs.** Applying color too soon and having to thoroughly wash and rinse the color out may cause unnecessary slippage and impede the locking process. For best results, your hair should be colored before the hair is loc'd. Because color applications can "roughen" the

cuticle, and it is easier to wash color out of loose hair, getting color *before* you loc is a better idea.

5. **Going too long in between retightening sessions when you have short hair.** Short hair, as well as loose hair, fly-aways, and areas that have experienced breakage will adapt faster to the locing process if they are retightened at least every four weeks. Regular, closer retightening timeframes help to ensure that the hair remains in the loc, and if it does slip out of the lock, you or your loctician will be able to put it back before the pattern slides out of your hair and the entire loc unravels.

6. **Believing that the traditional locing process does not apply to you.** Sisterlocks™, Nappylocs and Braidlocs can lend the feeling that you have "instant locs"! Your hair is perfectly sectioned, and you may even have considerable length. This feeling cannot be trusted. Although you will have slightly more freedom with handling your new locs, you should also be prepared for your hair to go through the same transitions that traditional locs go through. The different locing methods universally share the same attributes and challenges! The hair, whether afro-textured or wavy, will start off smoothly in the loc, then expand, frizz and eventually compact down into a mature loc.

Nappturous Diva's Solutions to the Top Five Mistakes Mature Sisterlock™, Nappylocs and Braidlocs Wearers Make:

1. **Not recognizing when to moisturize, and the importance of a hair-care routine that works for you**

A fabulous realization will one day occur for every loc wearer – the day when you realize that you have more mature locs than immature locs!

And then… you feel the ends of your locs, and they feel a little brittle. Your hair feels dry and it can't seem to retain moisture. It's time to incorporate more conditioning and/or moisturizing treatments, not just oils, into your hair routine.

Try light leave-in conditioning treatments, along with conditioning hair teas that are made with ingredients recommended in the homemade products section of this book.

2. **Forsaking your head scarf**

Ahhh, yes…the head scarf! Many Sisterlock™, Nappylocs and Braidlocs wearers of two years and longer are nodding their heads right about now! What are we agreeing about? Lint! Left unchecked, you'll look like you just came in from out in the snow!

Some of you may have had this problem from the very beginning! Remember to continue wrapping your hair with a silk, satin or polyester scarf at night.

Excellent choices include a satin bonnet that doesn't compact styles, Loc Pocket, Dreadsock™ and Loc Soc™ featured earlier in this book.

3. **Over-coloring**

It's so tempting to try new colors on the newfound length that you have experienced. If you do choose to color your locs, go to a loctician who is experienced in color, and kick your conditioning routine up a notch. Keep a close look out for any brittle ends or breakage. Never color in back-to-back sessions. If the color didn't turn out the way you wanted it to, remember the value you have in the health of your hair, and wait a few weeks.

If coloring is an absolute must, and you've already experienced the Henna route, explore newer ammonia-free organic options like Herbatint and Organic Color Systems.

4. Harsh self-retightenings

One of the main objections to Sisterlocks™, Nappylocs and Braidlocs is that "they are too expensive!" What people who make this comment may not realize is that all locs can be maintained at home once you learn how!

For Sisterlocks™, clients who have had their Sisterlocks™ for the recommended minimum of six months can take retightening classes. As you maintain your hair at home, work the tool carefully through your hair, as experience sometimes breeds rushing through your self-retightenings. You know you're a victim of rushing primarily if you have broken hairs around the base of your locs.

Nappylocs wearers learn how to retighten based on their booklet of information, and Braidlocs wearers can retighten using the simple latching technique described in the following pages.

Create time in your schedule and conduct your retightenings over the course of a week, a little at a time.

5. **Not realizing that texture still rules!**

Sisterlocks™, Nappylocs and Braidlocs greatly improve the overall durability of your hair, however, if you had fragile 4B natural hair **before** locs you will have fragile 4B locs **after** you are loc'd.

You should always treat your locs like you would handle a silk scarf – gently and carefully. Switch styles often, as that will help to reduce stress and potential breakage on the locs involved.

On the flip side, if your hair was a curly 3B before locs you'll have 3B locs that will curl on the ends until they mature. To combat slippage, bundle your hair when washing until you are comfortable that the slippage season is complete.

themethods**of**loc**maintenance**

How to Conduct a Traditional Retwisting and Palmrolling Session

Traditional loc maintenance or retwisting sessions can be conducted personally or by a Loctician. The method begins with clean, freshly washed locs.

1. Separate and clip the hair into four sections and ponytail off the section you are working on.

2. Pull down one loc, and using your aloe-oil mixture, or the Moisture Gloss homemade recipe, apply some to the root of the loc, and smooth a very small amount down the length of the loc. This mixture will not cause build up, and uses jojoba oil, which structurally mimics the natural

sebum of our hair, and 100% natural Aloe Vera, which is a natural moisturizer that heals and repairs.

3. Starting at the top of the loc, closest to your scalp, pull the new growth taunt, then twist and smooth the new growth in a clockwise direction.

4. Once you have twisted the new growth, place the loc in between the palms of your hands and roll the loc between your palms, moving your hands only in the direction that will continue the clockwise rotation. Do not go back and forth.

5. Once palmrolled, place a small hair clip at the base of the loc, securing the newly twisted new growth until it completely air dries. Additional locs can be added to the hair clip as they are completed.

Keep In Mind....

- You will see a certain amount of scalp showing after a loc maintenance session. Some people like this look, and others prefer a less manicured appearance. Loc maintenance can be conducted to produce a less manicured appearance by skipping #3 in the instructions prior and not twisting the root-beds of the locs. Palm rolling should still be conducted, because this will smooth the hairs into the loc over time, producing a stronger structural integrity.

- Refrain from over-twisting your hair and clipping it too tightly, as this will lend to thinning of the root-bed and breakage of the locs.

How To Latch your Traditional Locs or Braidlocs

Latching your locs entails using a latch hook to retighten the root-bed of your locs, instead of the twisting and palm rolling method. It is an easy way to maintain your locs if you have ever experienced your freshly twisted hair becoming untwisted with exercise, sleeping, shampooing or any of the other regular activities that cause your hair to unravel.

Latching can be done on any type of loc, including locs started with twists, braids or coils. As time progresses, you will not be able to tell the difference between a loc that has been maintained using a method different from the one used to start it. For many loc wearers who want immediate versatility without worrying about their hair, latching is easily done at home, and you can immediately wash your hair or manipulate your freshly tightened locs with no slippage of your new growth!

There are many different methods for latching hair, and I have seen people use everything from different sized latch hooks obtained from a craft store, to a hair pin! Try the options to find which one is easiest for you to work with.

Beginning Your Latching Session

Latching your hair personally saves money and can become a therapeutic experience. You have entered a realm of complete self-reliance when it comes to taking care of your hair, which can be freeing for those who started this journey reliant upon a stylist! The instructions provided here are specifically for latching, but the basics of the technique are also applicable to those who are conducting Sisterlock™ retightening sessions for themselves as well.

1. Divide your locs into four sections, clip the sections you will be working on later to the side with hair clips.

2. Place a ponytail holder around the section you are working on, and pull down one loc out of the ponytail. This will keep the neighboring locs secured, and is easier to use than hair clips since you can't see the area you're working on!

3. Taking one loc, smooth the new growth at the base by gently pulling it and twisting it one-half of a rotation in a clock-wise direction. This will help all of the loose hairs to be caught in the loc, reducing frizziness and resulting in a smoother, stronger, more compact loc.

4. Slowly insert the loop of the latch hook into the new growth located the **closest** to the base of the loc. Enter the new growth so that the loop of the tool exits closest to the base of the hair that is actually loc'd. You will be working your way **towards the scalp**, so ensure that your tool is positioned high in the new growth.

4. Once the loop of the latch hook has exited the other side of the new growth, lay the end of the loc on top of the latch hook, and insert the end into the hook by opening the latch and then closing it once the end of the loc is secure. One hand should be holding the latch hook, and the other hand should be holding the end of the loc.

5. Slowly let go of the end of the loc while pulling the latch hook back through the same way you entered the loc. You will be pulling the end of the loc out of the new growth in the same direction as the entrance of the tool.

6. Pull the loc through completely with your tool, and then use your fingers to give it a gentle, yet taunt pull to ensure that the loc has made it completely through the new growth.

7. Rotate around the base of the loc in a **clockwise** manner, repeating the same procedure. Inserting your latch hook into the new growth, enter **first through the left, then the top, the right and the bottom sides** of the locs' new growth. If you continued entering and exiting in the same direction, you would create spaces in your loc. The rotation ensures solid development of your locs. Enter through the bottom of the loc last, so that the locs will all lay in the same direction when you're done, towards the back of your head.

As you latch your locs, remember a few tips that will assist you in getting the results you desire. **Keep in mind…**

- Leave a small amount of new growth at the base of the loc so that you aren't putting too much stress on the hair follicles. Latching too tightly may cause your head to ache, and the only way to get relief is to wait a few days as your hair grows!
- If you are unable to make a full counter-clockwise rotation around the loc when you latch, you do not yet have enough new growth, and should wait a little longer between your latching sessions. Increase the time between your sessions by a week at a time until you

can make a full rotation. Making a full rotation around the loc increases the integrity of the loc, making it more solid and even as the months of latching go by.

· Pull the loc solidly through the base as you latch. Do not leave any bumps or knots in the loc, as these will promote potential breaking points in your loc, particularly if your locs are small in diameter.

· Use a ponytail holder and hair clips to ensure that neighboring locs are not getting caught in your tool, as you could attach two locs together!

· Conduct your latching sessions as often as you determine is necessary. This will depend on how much new growth you like to see. If your locs are small, however, latching sessions should be conducted no longer than every eight weeks, as smaller locs are more prone to breakage

· It is easier to latch your hair when it is slightly damp, so spray your hair with water or your Bedhead Growth spray as you latch.

Nappturous Diva Breaks It Down: Answers to Common Questions about Locs

Question #1- How Often do I Need to Conduct Loc Maintenance?

Answer: Your hair regime of choice for locs should still be conducted weekly, and the locs should be washed for health reasons. Freeformed locs are not maintenance free, but they are very low maintenance! For locs started with braids, coils or two-strand twists, maintain your locs using the palm rolling or latching methods. After the initial installation of your locs, the first wash should take place after the locs have "set", after approximately four to six weeks. Between the first four to six weeks, scalp cleansing should take place during this time if necessary, by applying a solution of eight ounces of water and ten drops of tea tree oil to a cotton ball, and rubbing the scalp thoroughly. Typical retwisting or retightening appointments should be set every 4-8 weeks, depending on the thickness and texture of the hair.

Question #2- How do I Keep the Lint Out of My Locs?

Answer: You'll find that your locs can sometimes be like Velcro – they attract lint! Lint in your locs is usually obtained when you are sleeping on fabrics that have particles that get trapped in your hair. This is an easily preventable problem that is rectified by tying your hair in a silk scarf or nylon-poly blend head wrap at night. If you already have lint in your hair, you can remove it gently by using tweezers, and take further precaution by sleeping on a satin pillowcase!

Question #3 – Is it Possible for Me to Take My Locs Out?

Answer: Locs are a style that, when installed, is meant to be permanent. The more appropriate question is "How do you transition from locs back to natural hair?"

Contrary to popular belief, locs that have not yet matured can be picked out. There have been Sisterlock™ wearers of up to 8 months into the journey who didn't care for the size of their locs, picked their Sisterlocks™ out of their hair and got them re-installed in a different size. Obviously, this takes a very long time, and should only be undertaken by someone who feels as though they will not be able to abide with their current choice of locs.

The closer you get to the ends of the hair, the more mature the loc will be, because the hair closer to the scalp has been recently twisted or tightened and has not yet loc'd. It is not usually necessary to cut all of your hair off, but the longer you have been loc'd, the more of the mature ends you will have to trim. Most people who transition from locs to natural hair and want to save as much hair as possible will commit the days and sometimes weeks it takes to slowly pick through semi-loc'd hair in order to release it from the loc. To make the process easier, recruit help and divide the job over a longer period of time. Any way you approach it, you will need to be committed to the removal process!

Question #4 – What Products Do I Need to Start Locs?

Answer: For freeform locs, you will need a natural, preferably residue-free shampoo and towel. For all cultivated locs, with the exception of Sisterlocks™, you will also need the Moisture Gloss homemade recipe or other light, clear, oil based product, residue-free shampoo, a comb with a tail for separating or parting the hair, and hair clips. For maintenance later on in your locing process, you will need your tool of choice for retightening, be it your hands, a latch hook or patented tool. Waxes, including beeswax and vegetable waxes, as well as shea and cocoa butters or "dreading gels" are not necessary. Because you are no longer combing your hair, it will naturally loc through the matting process described in the Four Stages of Locing.

Question #5 - How Much Time Does it Take to Grow Long Locs?

Answer: The answer depends on the normal growth rate of your hair. As you feed your hair through proper nutrition and take care of it through regular grooming, you will create the optimal conditions for your locs to grow. Multivitamins and hair supplements, healthy eating, regular washing and moisturization all contribute to healthy hair. Locs, just like a loose style, will become dry and brittle without moisture and the ends will break off. Healthy locs are the result of all of the above! A random number of hairs will at all times naturally go through a three stage growth cycle - anagen, telogen and catagen.

Anagen is the active growing phase that is also described as the "shooting" phase. The cells of the hair are dividing quickly and moving a new hair up through the hair follicle, while pushing the old hair out. Genetics determines how long this cycle will last, but it is typically two to six years.

Telogen is the resting phase, which comprises approximately 10% of your hair at any given time. The white bulb on the end that you see if you pull out a hair in the telogen phase is what is being formed at this time. Your hair stays in this phase for about 1/3 of a year.

The last stage is the catagen phase, in which 3% of your hair is cycling through, where the hair ceases growth and the outer root sheath shrinks and attaches itself to the root of the hair.

The hairs that are in the anagen phase cause anywhere between 25 and 100 strands to be shed every day. These hairs would normally fall out when you brush or comb your hair, but because your hair is loc'd, they become trapped in the matrix of the loc, and cause it to continue to grow longer. The ends of long loc'd hair are not attached to the scalp – they are primarily shed hairs that have grown into the loc. This is why it is important to ensure that the root-beds of your locs are comprised of enough hairs so that when your hair cycles through these phases, you maintain healthy locs.

Question #6 - Is it possible to Loc a Child's Hair?

Answer: Absolutely! Once the child is old enough to care for their own hair, they can make the decision to keep or cut their locs, but while you are responsible for their hair, that is your decision. Locs are easy to take care of and very conducive to an active child's lifestyle.

Sisterlocks™ are very popular for children because of their increased styling capabilities and versatility. The small size holds curls longer and can be clipped into small bows and store bought hair ornaments. Parents who want their child to have Sisterlocks™ or other small sized locs are advised to wait until the child is at least 7 years old, because their head is still growing and an otherwise square part can become rectangular over time.

Question #7 - Can a Broken Loc be Repaired?

Answer: Broken locs, whether small or large can be repaired easily. If one of your locs breaks off, keep the end that has broken. Trim any stray hairs off of the broken end of the loc and off of the loc that is still attached to your head. Obtain a sewing needle and thread that matches the color of your hair, thread the needle, and sew the loc back on. Trim the loose thread. The thread may be visible when holding the singular loc up, but eventually, the location where it was sewn will mesh within the loc, and no one will be able to tell that it has been repaired.

Question #8 - Should Locs be Conditioned?

Answer: It is a common misconception that locs do not need moisture or conditioning. It is true that thick creams that are based in shea butter do not need to be applied to locs, particularly while they are maturing, but you are not limited to these types of conditioners! Nourish your locs with water, which is the ultimate moisturizer, and infuse it with essential oils, herbs and a carrier oil, as in the Bedhead Growth spray recipe. One of my favorite loc conditioners is the Herb Infused Hair Tea, where the conditioning properties of the herbs are contained in the water, and the solution is poured over the locs, for a clean, light conditioner. Locs love Aloe Vera gel and castor oil, which makes them softer to the touch and produces a beautiful sheen. Moisturizing your loc keeps the hairs healthy and stronger, for healthier, stronger locs.

Question #9 - Can Different Methods of Maintaining Locs be Combined?

Answer: Yes, different methods of maintenance can be combined, but it is advisable to choose one method and stick with it. If you decide to change methods, the primary concern that most loc wearers express is, "Will you be able to see where I transitioned from one maintenance method to another?" The answer to that question is yes, in the beginning, but not so much over time. As time goes by, despite what method is used to maintain the locs, the natural coiling and matting process of your hair will produce a cylindrically shaped loc.

The Best Free Sources for Natural Hair & Loc Information

Still want more answers, ideas and support? The natural hair community is active and open to giving you what you need. Check it out!

NaturalSuccessNetwork.com: A social network created for women of color, discussing everything from hair, to family, to keeping it all in balance!

Nappturality.com This is one of the most popular, largest and content-rich forums available, with plenty of articles, user-friendly documents and ideas, as well as friendly, supportive members! Nappturality offers both free and paid membership options.

Nappyhairaffair.com An organization that facilitates hosted "Hair-Days" around the country. Learn how to host your own Hair Day support group in your area. Join as a member and become part of a like-minded group making an impact on future generations. Receive consistent affirmations on the cultural impact of natural hair, designed to develop positive self-esteem.

Naturallyyoumagazine.com The first natural hair magazine for women, Naturally You! is the premier natural hair infotainment resource, featuring large, vibrant pictures and how-to instructions. This magazine can be conveniently ordered and read online or delivered to your mailbox!

Ymib.com This natural lifestyle magazine is for those who want to experience more than just natural hair. Get the latest on what's happening in the natural community with an urban, boho flair!

Diasporahaircare.com This site offers a natural hair care forum with over 20 boards in which you can participate, obtain support and find answers to any hair concerns! Free and paid membership options are available.

Longhaircareforum.com This hair care forum is specifically for those who want to develop long hair and includes women with all types of hair, including natural and locs.

Motowngirl.com Practical instructions for how to work with nappy, kinky and curly hair, as well as natural hair articles, tips, recipes, product reviews and how-to information are bountiful on this "all-in-one" site!

Ourhair.net An extensive forum with informative articles for those who wish to join a community of natural hair wearers.

Mynatural.com This site includes user reviews of natural hair products. Find lists of any hair care product you could imagine to review, from essential oils to commercial products!

Going-Natural.com This forum-based site is filled with educational links about natural products, natural people and natural styles.

Palacinka.com A product-user review site for naturally textured women of color. Read reviews and post your own!

Sistasplace.biz At sistasplace.biz, you can read reviews and also purchase products for natural hair. Unlike some stores, sistasplace.biz also lists the ingredients in the products offered, allowing you to make an educated decision.

NaturalHairDigest.com This fun e-zine and web resource is dedicated to the best natural hair has to offer online, and known for its scrumptious homemade recipes for hair care.

NaturallyCurly.com You can find the latest in hair care information on this site that allows visitors to rate products. Join their forum, CurlTalk™, and read articles from authors including Linda "Mosetta" Jones in the CurlColumn!

Tytecurl.com This site stores a host of articles and features a column by our In-House Expert Anita Grant! The site is designed to provide education, empowerment and management information for natural women.

Afrobella.com Patrice Yursik is the author of this informational and fun to read blog about natural hair, products and the trials and celebrations that go along with both!

Natural Hair Yahoo Groups

Yahoo groups are an excellent way to learn more information about natural hair as well as gain any support, ideas or simply have fun with a family of people who understand exactly what you are experiencing! To join any of the groups below, insert the group name where it says "groupname" exactly as you see it below into the following email address, and the moderator will email you with more information on how to join. The email address is: groupname-subscribe@yahoogroups.com. If you already have a yahoo username and password, you can go to Groups on yahoo.com and search by the group name below to join.

NaturalGrooming: A group for Black people who want to talk about grooming and maintaining natural hair.

LockItUp: The largest collection of Sisterlocks™ photos on the Internet. The group provides excellent advice and support to "newbies", to Sisterlocks™. "Lurkers", those who are still deciding if Sisterlocks™ is the way for them to go, are welcome.

Natural_Hair_and_Black Women: Members of this list talk about going natural, staying natural, and having fun with it in the meantime. You'll learn tips for care, styling, and maintenance.

LovinLocks: LovinLocks is an open forum to discuss locs, dreadlocs, nubian locs, organic locs, Sisterlocks™, Brotherlocks, Braidlocs, Nappylocks, and any other kind of locs and natural hair.

LockCity: A Yahoo Group created for anyone who wants information, discussion, encouragement, advice and to share their stories about wearing locs.

BlackTresses: Members include Black women and men who have made the decision to stop altering the natural structure of their hair.

LadyLocs: This forum was started for Black women who have locs or are thinking about getting locs. Women with natural hair or those thinking about going natural are also welcome to post.

Nappturous Diva's Principle #3

We Know Our Ingredients

Our hair is, in part, our own creation. The extent that we feed our hair internally and externally with ingredients in the products that we use shapes the health and condition of our hair. We use products that have ingredients that support the greatest good of our hair.

Products…Know Your Ingredients!

Before we can talk about what products to use, we need to talk about what's IN the products we use. I know you may be tempted to skip this section, but a foundation for your hair is being built here, and you want healthy hair right?

Please read on for your health! Later on, you will find that my recommended products may not be something that you can easily find in the grocery or your local BSS (Beauty Supply Store).

I believe that we need to completely, openly and freely accept the full gift of empowerment that goes with being natural, and here's why…

Back In The Day…

One day when I was newly natural, I was happily enjoying my wash and condition routine, when I had a sudden thought amidst the soapy bubbles running down my face.

Why go through all the effort to get rid of chemicals and be natural, if I was just going to put chemical-laden products on my hair and scalp? I knew from research that my scalp is one of the most porous areas of skin on my body. Did I really want potentially toxic chemicals absorbing through my skin? It just made sense, so I began researching the products that I was using for personal care.

An interesting fact that I found was that most of my products contained several different chemical ingredients that were potentially harmful, toxic and/or carcinogenic (cancer-causing).

This may not seem to be of immediate concern because the ingredients may be used in small quantities, however, looking at the combined effect of using 5-10 or more of these products for personal care every day, I figured that I was unnecessarily exposing myself to anywhere between 50-100 toxic and potentially hazardous ingredients, creating a dangerous "chemical cocktail."

How much is too much?

I really didn't know, and didn't want to find out by using products containing these ingredients when natural options that work just as well or better are available!

According to the FDA, **"under the Federal Food, Drug, and Cosmetic (FD&C) Act, cosmetics and their ingredients are not required to undergo approval before they are sold to the public.** John Bailey, Ph.D., Director of FDA's Office of Cosmetics and Colors, says **'Consumers believe that if it's on the market, it can't hurt me, and this belief is sometimes wrong."**

To quickly research the products you are using, the most complete reference that I've found is the database of the non-profit research and advocacy organization, Environmental Working Group.

The organization analyzed 7,093 ingredients in 14,835 personal care products and then cross-referenced their list against chemicals listed in 37 toxicity and regulatory databases. One of the most interesting findings is that **Ultra Sheen,** a product line specifically for African-American hair care is number one their list of Highest Concern Brands!

15

harmfulingredient**review**

Sometimes, you won't have the opportunity to research every product before you buy it, and you'll need to learn how to read the ingredient list. In my review of over 50 of the most popular and widely used commercial products from Internet, grocery and beauty supply stores; I've assembled a Quick Reference Guide for you.

Nappturous Diva's Top Red Flag Ingredients Commonly Used in Black Hair Care Products

The following list names the ingredient, what it is or how it's used, and why you should be concerned.

#1 Glycols (the entire group of) – Moisturizer, Glycerin substitute

Did cause liver abnormalities and kidney damage in laboratory animals. Chronic exposure to the glycol ethers in humans results in fatigue, lethargy, nausea, anorexia, tremors, and anemia

#2 Parabens (the entire group of) - Most common preservative used, found primarily in creams & lotions, petroleum based

Parabens are capable of sensitizing skin and inducing cutaneous allergic responses. Immune system toxicants, classified as toxic

#3 Polyquaternim (with any number following) - Film forming, gives an impression of softness

May cause dermatitis, skin irritant

#4 Mineral Oil - Petroleum by-product that coats the skin

Non-toxic, however, interferes with skins ability to eliminate toxins, promoting acne and other disorders. Slows down skin function and cell development

#5 Sodium Lauryl Sulfate also, Sodium Laureth Sulfate (SLS) - In shampoos and conditioners, used to create a lather

Causes dermatitis, safety limits on use/purity/manufacturing

#6 Formaldehyde, a.k.a. DMDM hydantoin, MDM hydantoin, Formalin - Colorless gas with vapors that are extremely irritating to mucous membranes

Reproductive/developmental toxicity, cancer hazard and probable carcinogen, causes skin irritation, not safe inhaled as in aerosolized products

#7 Coal Tar, a.k.a. FD, FDC or FD&C color - In products designed to treat dandruff & flaky scalp

Known human carcinogen, may contain harmful impurities or form toxic breakdown in products

#8 Propylene Glycol - Most common moisture-carrying vehicle other than water

Immune system toxicants (allergies, sensitization), strongly de-greases and dries the skin

#9 Polymers – Silicone, Dimethicone or Cyclomethicone - Light-reflecting chemicals which bind to the hair surface Used to form a glossy reflection and claim to protect the hair

Although non-toxic, be careful with any ingredient that forms a coating on the hair and scalp. This can potentially cause it to be more difficult for the scalp to breathe and release natural oils to the hair

As you see, besides being considered toxic, harsh on the hair and bad for your overall health, almost every single one of these ingredients contributes to one of the primary hair problems cited by black women – dry hair.

Dryness can facilitate dandruff, and dry scalp, which, if left unchecked, leads to damaged hair. Dry hair can also cause damaged hair, which breaks off and leads people to believe their hair cannot grow. Enter problem number two– "slow" hair growth. It is amazing how many African-American women believe their hair doesn't grow. The truth is our hair grows about ½ inch every month. For most people, it's simply a matter of how much of that hair growth you actually keep!

Damaged hair is a problem with one common solution, that being a good trim – or for some, a cut. I'm having flashbacks now of all the trims that turned out to be haircuts! We don't want to loose the growth that we've worked hard for and you'll see your hair growth faster when you protect and shield your hair from damage.   Condition, condition, condition.   Wear protective styles and condition some more. All these issues take us right back to the Principles of a Nappturous Diva!

Despite the references that are listed here, you may decide that you still want to use products that contain the ingredients listed above. I believe each person should do what they feel is best for them.

This information is meant to empower and educate, and I encourage you to continue to use all the information you've gathered on your journey to develop your idea of what works for you!

nappturousdiva'slusciouslist
Of Recommended Products

I've been mixing products in my bathroom since Whitney and Bobby were each at the top of the charts and it was cool to wear spandex outside, even though we weren't exercising! That was a long time ago, and these days, it is great to have so many options of nature-based, non-toxic commercial products that are manufactured by caring companies, as well as homemade versions that actually save money in the long run!

Although this is definitely not an all-inclusive list, I personally have given each of these products a five-star rating. For all the product-junkie Nappturous Divas, remember, natural hair is simple – you don't need a lot of products to have beautiful, soft healthy hair. This list is quite extensive, however, to allow for options if you wish to change your hair routine and need suggestions. If you

do not see your favorite product here, I have probably checked it out and it's not listed for a

reason…see Principle #3. Enjoy!

Favorite Commercial Products

Shampoos

Company: Dr. Bronner's

Where to Find: Natural Food Stores, www.drbronner.com, 1.877.786.3649

Nappturous Divas FAVS: **Peppermint Pure-Castile Soap**, used as shampoo.

Comes in a variety of formulations, including: almond, baby-mild, tea tree*, peppermint* and eucalyptus.

Features: The peppermint and tea tree are great to use for dry scalp, and the baby-mild is good for adults and children, as well as those with sensitive skin. Dilute the product with water 5-10:1 in a separate spray bottle before using.

Company: Sisterlocks™

Where to Find: www.sisterlocks.com

Nappturous Divas FAVS: **Starter Shampoo** for beginning locs

Features: The Starter Shampoo is pH balanced to help hair "grab to begin the locking process" while still leaving hair soft. Good for all locs.

Company: Shea Moisture

Where to Find: www.sheamoisture.com

Nappturous Divas FAVS: **Raw Shea Butter Moisture Retention Shampoo, Coconut & Hibiscus Curl Control Shampoo, African Black Soap Deep Conditioning Shampoo**

Features: Nature-based shampoos and hair washes that combine a foundation of natural ingredients and aloe vera for a conditioning, gentle hair wash.

Company: Karen's Body Beautiful

Where to Find: www.karensbodybeautiful.com

Nappturous Divas FAVS: **Karen's Body Beautiful Conditioning Shampoo**

Features: Customized fragrances and soft results. What more could a girl ask for?

Company: Organikah

Where to Find: www.organikah.com

Nappturous Divas FAVS: **Herbal Shampoo**

Features: Wonderful poo containing coconut, jojoba and olive oils, moisturizing honey and protein.

Company: Blended Beauty

Where to Find: www.blended-beauty.com

Nappturous Divas FAVS: **Soy Cream Shampoo**

Features: Creating a sudsy clean feeling, this pH-balanced shampoo is enriched with silk protein, soy, and grapeseed oil.

*Both the tea tree and peppermint Dr. Bronner's and the Ebene Naturals Tea Tree and Lavender are good for dry scalp or dandruff.

Conditioners/Deep Conditioners/Pre-Poo Treatments

Company: Burt's Bees

Where to Find: www.burtsbees.com

Nappturous Divas FAVS: **Avocado Butter Pre-Shampoo Hair Treatment**

Features: Vegetable glycerin mixed with olive and avocado oils for moisturizing makes for a very thick paste that is excellent for pre-poos! Can be diluted with a carrier oil for easier spreading.

Company: Anita Grant

Where to Find: www.anitagrant.com

Nappturous Divas FAVS: **Rhassoul Deep Condish**

Features: Unrefined black cocoa butter and soya based vitamin E cubes that require minimal preparation to use. The yummy result is hair that is amazingly soft and fluffy like a cloud!

Company: Karen's Body Beautiful

Where to Find: www.karensbodybeautiful.com

Nappturous Divas FAVS: **Luscious Locks Moisturizing Hair Mask**

Features: Contains essential ingredients to promote hair growth, like nettle and rosemary, and deep conditions with aloe. Thick and rich!

Company: My HoneyChild Natural Products

Where to Find: www.myhoneychild.com

Nappturous Divas FAVS: **Honey and Horsetail Reconstructor**

Features: Super-rich reconstructing conditioner, excellent for restoring moisture to dry, colored or damaged hair. Wonderful fragrance!

Company: Carol's Daughter

Where to Find: www.carolsdaughter.com

Nappturous Divas FAVS: **Tui Shea Butter Hair Smoothie**

Features: This conditioning treatment uses a rich combination of shea and cocoa butters and jojoba oil for intense moisture treatment!

Company: Kinky-Curly

Where to Find: www.kinky-curly.com

Nappturous Divas FAVS: **Knot Today**

Features: Detangling herbal condition with horsetail, wild cherry bark and marshmallow root, can also be used as a leave- in conditioner.

Company: Organikah

Where to Find: www.organikah.com

Nappturous Divas FAVS: **Shea Butter Conditioner**

Features: Simple and effective moisturizing conditioner with sweet almond oil and shea.

Company: Shea Moisture

Where to Find: www.sheamoisture.com

Nappturous Divas FAVS: **African Black Balancing Conditioner, Yucca & Baobob Volumizing Conditioner**

Features: Made with ingredients like coconut oil, shea butter and aloe vera, these products add moisture and improve overall hair condition.

Rinses

Company: Ebene Naturals

Where to Find: www.ebenenaturals.com

Nappturous Divas FAVS: **Conditioning Herbal Hair Rinse**

Features: This product is made up of loose dried conditioning leaves and herbs and comes with a muslin bag, which is then seeped in warm water to make a tea for the hair. Excellent infusion of natural conditioners and is a purifying rinse for the hair.

Company: Ebene Naturals

Where to Find: www.ebenenaturals.com

Nappturous Divas FAVS: **Herbal Vinegar Rinse**

Features: Liquid product combining apple cider vinegar, herbs, EO's and vitamins. Perfect for dry scalp and/or product build-up removal, helps to restore natural ph balance.

Leave In Conditioners/Moisturizers

Light Moisturizing Creams

Company: Karen's Body Beautiful

Where to Find: www.karensbodybeautiful.com

Nappturous Divas FAVS: **Karen's Body Beautiful Hair Milk,** My fav fragrances: Vanilla Latte and White Tea, 24 total fabulous fragrances

Features: Fascinating results after one use! Is light enough to use daily on both natural hair and locs.

Company: Anita Grant

Where to Find: www.anitagrant.com

Nappturous Divas FAVS: **Whipped Butter** in Lemon Sponge Cake

Features: Refreshingly light whipped hair butter smells good enough to eat! Non-greasy and good for regular use. Soaks in like you wouldn't believe!

Company: Sisterlocks™

Where to Find: www.sisterlocks.com

Nappturous Divas FAVS: **Moisture Treatment**

Features: Hair literally soaks up the Jojoba oil and essential oils in this conditioning leave- in treatment. Great for Sisterlocks, traditional locks and for natural hair too! Store in fridge.

Company: Organikah

Where to Find: www.organikah.com

Nappturous Divas FAVS: **Whipped Hair Butter**

Features: The label says it's light, and it really is! Soft and fluffy, this product smoothes on and leaves hair moist but non-greasy!

Company: Alaffia

Where to Find: www.alaffia.com

Nappturous Divas FAVS: **Shea and Virgin Coconut Enriching Hair Lotion**

Features: Named ingredients along with B5 and wheat protein improve softness and elasticity while encouraging growth with Rooibos Tea Extract.

Company: Anita Grant

Where to Find: www.anitagrant.com

Nappturous Divas FAVS: **Creamy Café Latte**

Features: A detangler and leave in conditioner, this creamy concoction smoothes dry tresses and smells beautiful.

Company: Karen's Body Beautiful

Where to Find: www.karensbodybeautiful.com

Nappturous Divas FAVS: **Karen's Body Beautiful Hair Butter**

Features: Melts into hair, and leaves a luscious fragrance and feel.

Company: Ebene Naturals

Where to Find: www.ebenenaturals.com

Nappturous Divas FAVS: **Essential Hair Butter**

Features: Definitely rich and creamy, this hair butter provides needed help to dry, damaged or brittle hair. Great for moisturizing when everything else seems to evaporate!

Water based EO Sprays

Company: Zum Mist

Where to Find: www.shopzilla.com

Nappturous Divas FAVS: **Refreshing Spray,** Lavender-Mint, Rosemary-Mint, Lavender-Lemon, and other fragrances

Features: Made with purified water, essential and fragrance oil, and aloe and vegetable glycerin, this mist is excellent to carry about for refreshing your hair and scalp on the go!

Company: Oyin Handmade

Where to Find: www.oyinhandmade.com

Nappturous Divas FAVS: **Greg Juice**

Features: A delightful mix of spring water infused with EO's, vegetable glycerin and Aloe Vera juice. Use for detangling and for adding moisture. Easily dilute with water if necessary, and use daily for flexibility and protective styling.

Hair Growth and Scalp Treatments

Company: High Performance Organics

Where to Find: www.hpospatreatments.com

Nappturous Divas FAVS: **Happy Scalp**

Features: A mixture of peppermint and spearmint essential oils, you can use the medicine dropper to apply just the right amount to the scalp. Massage in as part of your pre-poo or use afterwards when moisturizing for a vibrant scalp!

Company: Anita Grant

Where to Find: www.anitagrant.com

Nappturous Divas FAVS: **Organic Sapote Fruit Seed Oil**

Features: This simple cold-pressed oil has a natural cherry fragrance and has been credited with assisting in hair growth. Also excellent as an everyday oil, restoring sheen and moisture.

Company: Shea Moisture

Where to Find: www.sheamoisture.com

Nappturous Divas FAVS: **African Black Soap Dandruff & Dry Scalp Elixer**

Features: Reduces dry scalp and flaking while soothing and balancing the scalp with aloe vera, salicylic acid and tea tree oil.

Company: Carol's Daughter

Where to Find: www.carolsdaughter.com

Nappturous Divas FAVS: **Lisa's Hair Elixir**

Features: Soy, sweet almond and corn oil create a medium weight oil that is infused with sage, rosemary and peppermint, excellent for dry scalp, dandruff and restoring freshness to the hair.

Oils

Company: Ebene Naturals

Where to Find: www.ebenenaturals.com

Nappturous Divas FAVS: **Conditioning Styling Oil Spray**

Features: A light oil with moisturizing agents. Comes in a spray bottle for even distribution.

Company: Curls

Where to Find: www.curls.biz

Nappturous Divas FAVS: **Pure Pomegranate Seed Oil Blend**

Features: This exotic oil adds sheen and helps with dry scalp conditions.

Company: Blended Beauty

Where to Find: www.blended-beauty.com

Nappturous Divas FAVS: **All Natural Hair Oil**

Features: A variety of healthy hair enhancing oils come together in a mixture that will seal moisture without clogging pores. Also can be used as a pre-poo hot oil treatment!

Styling Pomades/Creams/Gels

Company: Real Purity Natural Cosmetics

Where to Find: www.holisticbeauty.net

Nappturous Divas FAVS: **Real Hair Gel**

Features: Completely natural aloe-based hair gel that creates a soft hold!

Company: Aubrey Organics

Where to Find: www.holisticbeauty.net

Nappturous Divas FAVS: **Aubrey Organics Mandarin Magic Jelly**

Features: Moisturizes, adds shine and a medium hold while conditioning with Chinese herbs, panthenol and aloe vera!

Company: Ebene Naturals

Where to Find: www.ebenenaturals.com

Nappturous Divas FAVS: **Natural Styling Balm**

Features: Unique vegetable wax base provides no build-up, and is a great alternative to drying hair gels. Used on short or long hair, helps to control frizz and good for men and women. For all hair types.

Company: Kinky-Curly

Where to Find: www.kinky-curly.com

Nappturous Divas FAVS: **Curling Custard**

Features: Brings out the curls with a lightweight, moisturizing cream for gloss, hold and shine! Best results on 3A, B & C hair, but good for all hair types.

Company: Kinky-Curly

Where to Find: www.kinky-curly.com

Nappturous Divas FAVS: **Gloss Pomade**

Features: Increase shine and reduce frizz with this medium weight pomade. Best results on 3A, B & C hair, but good for all hair types.

Company: Blended Beauty

Where to Find: www.blended-beauty.com

Nappturous Divas FAVS: **Happy Nappy Styles**

Features: Highly textured hair will love this silky cream, excellent for defining two-strand twists or slicking hair into an updo or ponytail!

Children's Hair Products

All of Nappturous Diva's recommended products are safe and wonderful for use on children's hair; however, this section features additional products that are made specifically for children!

For Children

Company: Ebene Naturals

Where to Find: www.ebenenaturals.com

Nappturous Divas FAVS: **Little Princess Soy Conditioning Hairdress**

Features: Light weight, beautiful fragranced hair crème for little ones. Made with cocoa and shea butters, and includes vegetable wax, which does not leave build-up like beeswax. Great for slicking fly-aways into braids and ponytails!

Company: Blended Beauty

Where to Find: www.blended-beauty.com

Nappturous Divas FAVS: **Silky Swirls Shampoo, Tug-Me-Not Conditioner, Down & Out Styles, Soft Curls & Swirls, Butter Me Up, Satin Style Detangler, Jelly Cream**

Features: All of Blended Beauty's products for children stand out because they are uniquely ph balanced for sensitive scalps, and your children will love the wonderful scent they all share!

Favorite Products for Biracial Hair

A multitude of curls can bring a multitude of features that need special attention! Define curls, reduce frizz, and add moisture without weighing down 3A, B & C hair! The following companies produce products that are great for all types of hair, but are special favs of biracial Nappturous Divas!

Biracial Hair Products

Company: Kinky-Curly

Where to Find: www.kinky-curly.com

Nappturous Divas FAVS: **Knot Today, Curling Custard, Spiral Spritz, Gloss Pomade***

Features: Apply all four products for best results. See instructions on website.

Company: Curls

Where to Find: www.curls.biz

Nappturous Divas FAVS: **Curl Euphoria Elixir**

Features: As a high-sheen, medium weight pomade, this curl gloss is a great protectant for heat-styling.

Company: Blended Beauty

Where to Find: www.blended-beauty.com

Nappturous Divas FAVS: **Curly Frizz Pudding**

Features: Soft-hold aloe gel hair lotion that smoothes and defines each curl. Completely natural ingredients for bounce & shine!

Company: Blended Beauty

Where to Find: www.blended-beauty.com

Nappturous Divas FAVS: **Kicks For Curls**

Features: Light moisturizers and satiny conditioners create a spritz that revives squished or frizzed curls! Leaves hair super soft.

In-House Expert! The Mixtress Anita Grant, Owner and Creator of anitagrant.com

On "Fabulous Natural Products That Really Work!"

AnitaGrant.com was created on the 5th of December 2005, by the all round self-proclaimed-cosmetic-label -reader-ingredient junkie-mixtress, Anita. Rather than fill her creations with chemical brews, Anita works very closely with Mama Nature, utilizing only those quality ingredients that yield superior benefits for your RDA *(recommended daily application)*. Being accountable to her customers is something that is always on her mind, in her hair & on her skin. Anita Grant is a family owned business, providing deep condish treats, hair butters, skin smoothies & the power of moisture direct to your door!

Your business of making luscious products has really exploded, what do you think has caused this huge uptake? What makes Anita Grant products different?

Attitudes towards buying organic & fair trade goods are slowly changing here in the UK. Consumers are more label savvy today then they were say five years ago. I can't speak for the nation, but in my family it is a massive part of our life & well-being. The majority of my ingredients are produced & purchased directly from farming communities and/or partnerships I have with fair trade and organic ingredient suppliers throughout the world. It's a way to foster community, economic independence & cultural survival.

What makes my hair & skin care goodies different from the others - Perhaps the quality of my hair & skin care goodies, the origins of my ingredients, or maybe even the information on my website & blog. I'm not 100% sure, but I do know that whatever it is, people from all over the world like it.

More and more women are embracing their texture and moving towards natural (chemical-free) products; what are the top 3 Anita Grant products that you recommend for basic hair maintenance?

It really depends on the texture of each person's hair and their needs. One thing that I have learned is that not all natural hair is created the same. Everyone has at least 2 or 3 different textures associated with various patterns and lengths.

When looking for hair care products, I would advise your readers to use the same values as they would when they are shopping for food, as it DOES matter what we put on our hair and scalp.

In my humble opinion, I think that it is important for *all consumers* to educate themselves about the benefits of the ingredients contained within the bottles and jars & determine what is best for them.

170

The popularity of homemade products has increased dramatically, and more and more people are making their products. What are some of your insider secrets to making great products at home?

1. Research, research and more research the benefits of all the ingredients that are included within your mix.

2. Be happy when you're mixing.

3. Don't allow any negativity to enter into your mixture!

These are my 3 top recommendations.

Lately, there's been a lot of talk about how using products for hair maintenance could classify someone who doesn't have chemicals on her hair as "not natural". What's your definition of natural?

 Please allow me to begin by saying - Absolutely everything has a chemical & physical structure.

There is a fine line between what is "natural" and what is deemed to be natural and free from synthetically made ingredients, like silicones and polymers.

My definition of natural is "in it's purest form."

What's your personal Hair Care regime?

I like to keep it simple.

I wash my hair once a week with my Babassu Shampoo, condition rinse with an infusion of herbs, give my hair the spa treatment with my Rhassoul Deep Condish cubes once a month, and depending on the style of the day, I dab a little Whipped Butter or Organic Sapote Seed Oil from root to tip, as it locks in the moisture. I vary this a lot with a combination of my hair goodies but it really depends on how my hair is feeling on the day.

17

nappturousdiva'**slusciouslist**
Of Natural Homemade Products

How to Make Luscious, Effective Products Easily!

Have you ever wondered what really was in that special secret mixture that your Natural Hair Stylist uses at the salon? Do you like experimenting with products? At least 70% of all Nappturous Divas who are reading this book have to admit to turning their bathroom into their own product laboratory at least once during their natural hair journey!

When I originally opened my natural hair salon, I wasn't able to find a good hair moisturizer, so I made one of my own, and began my quest to find, try, test on myself (and others!) as well as understand natural ingredients. After months of research, I finally understood the development, combination and pricing of many of the therapeutic ingredients that can be combined to make products that smelled great and addressed the issues of a varied clientele.

Making your own products is not as daunting as it may seem, especially if you can follow a simple recipe. Many times, you may find that it is cheaper in the long run to make your own products, versus purchasing commercial products! It's fun and easy, and as you develop more experience, you may find that your products have legs of their own, as they will mysteriously walk off to your best friend's bathroom and mother's cabinet! I usually set aside one Sunday every other month to whip up a few batches of homemade shampoo bars, hair creams and other products.

Once you have the basic ingredients, and an understanding of how to preserve your products, you can mix large batches of product and store it to be used at your convenience. Ensure that the ingredients you use have a shelf life that is conducive to the time in which you want to use your product, and that you follow proper storage requirements that are listed on the labels of the ingredients.

Here's some beginning terminology to help you as you try some of the recipes that I've seen work

wonders on a variety of hair types.

Essential Oil (EO) – A plant oil that is most commonly extracted from the leaves and flowers of a

plant primarily through distillation, but cold pressing or solvent extraction are used in some cases.

A 100% pure, therapeutic Grade A essential oil should not be confused with a carrier oil, and is

not oily to the touch.

Because they are concentrated, essential oils can be as much as 50 to 70 times more

therapeutically potent than the plants they are derived from, so please read any instructions for

use carefully. With the preparation of your products, you will most commonly add these pure,

sometimes organic oils to a carrier oil for use. Store your essential oils in a cool location, away

from light, heat (including microwaves) and humidity, which can cause your oils to age

prematurely and retain little therapeutic value.

Carrier Oil (CO or base oil)– A vegetable, nut or seed oil, used in personal care products to

dilute essential oils. Carrier oils have skin nourishing qualities of their own, and have are oily to

the touch. This type of ingredient will form most of the majority of product recipes

Fragrance Oil (FO, aroma oil, aromatic oil) – A blend of synthetic aromas used to add scent to cosmetic preparations. Fragrance oils usually are less expensive than an essential oil due to their man-made qualities.

Ayurvedic Herb Oils- Ayurvedic treatments are based on a system of ancient healthcare native to the Indian subcontinent. Ayurveda roughly translated means "knowledge of life". Ayurvedic oil is created by steeping a special selection of ayurvedic herbs in water to create a strong herbal infusion. This water is then added to oil, usually sesame or coconut oil, and the oil is then gently warmed until all of the moisture is evaporated.

Shelf Stable – A product that typically would require refrigeration, which has been chemically altered so that it can be safely stored at room temperature for longer periods of time, usually not exceeding one year.

Viscosity – The properties of a product that resist force, causing the product to flow.

Tools you'll need to make your products at home

Select the tools for the product you are making from the list below. Typically, you won't need all of these tools for one recipe!

- A clear working area

- Eye droppers for measuring small amounts of ingredient

- Essential oils, unrefined butters and CO's, herbs and any other ingredients for your recipe

- Double boiler or makeshift warmer (small glass bowl that can sit inside a larger glass bowl)

- Spatulas

- Glass measuring cups

- Glass or ceramic mixing bowls

- Hand mixer

- Glass storage containers, products with EO's in them will store longer

- Molds for your soap products

- Ball or mesh strainer for straining herbs

- Paper towels, Viva works well due to a cloth-like durability

Sterilize each tool in a pot of boiling water at 150 degrees Fahrenheit or a dishwasher before proceeding. If using a dishwasher, select the sterilization option, and do not add any dishwashing detergent. Wipe your storage containers clean with a paper towel doused in a natural spray of eight ounces of distilled water with 10 drops of tea tree oil or alcohol. We're going to be using ingredients that you have hand selected for quality, and you will want your tools to help you preserve their therapeutic nature.

Many of these basic ingredients I've listed to help you get started in making your own product, you might think you have found in your local BSS (Beauty Supply Store). For example, one product might read "Tea Tree Oil" or "Shea Butter". However, if you happen to read the ingredient label, either the featured ingredient is not the first ingredient listed, or in some cases, one of the LAST ingredients on the label!

If you're paying for what you think is 100% pure shea butter, or a 100% essential oil, ensure that that's what you're getting by reading the label. For that reason, I recommend going to your local natural food store or trusted online carrier of natural products for your ingredients instead.

However, we must remember the guiding principle of this chapter, Nappturous Divas' Principle #3 – We Know Our Ingredients! The reason we know our ingredients is because we read and research the listings on the ingredient label! As you learn more about the therapeutic nature of the various ingredients and develop a relationship with your hair, you'll be able to combine different ingredients to customize a product to your specific hair requirements! I've compiled a basic list of some of the most effective natural ingredients for you to use to make both your everyday and select luxurious hair preparations.

Carrier Oils

Avocado

Description: Heavy weight, usually diluted with other carrier oils

Benefit: Nutrient rich with vitamins A, C, D and E. Contains proteins and works well at moisturizing dry skin and hair. Non-greasy, and is said to stimulate hair growth.

Jojoba

Description: Medium weight, liquid wax extracted from the jojoba bean. Classified as a vegetable oil.

Benefit: Most closely resembles human sebum, therefore highly penetrative.

Grapeseed

Description: Light weight, thin and odorless.

Benefit: Contains vitamins including E, C and beta-carotene. Good for skin irritations.

Coconut (virgin)

Description: Light weight once melted; should have a slight, natural coconut fragrance.

Benefit: High in saturated fats and easily absorbed. Also highly moisturizing, silky, and helps to reduce protein loss.

Olive (Extra-Virgin)

Description: Medium weight with an earthy fragrance.

Benefit: Contains vitamins A, E and saturated fats. Nourishes, conditions and improves elasticity of the hair, promoting softness and sheen.

Castor

Description: Medium weight and odorless.

Benefit: Castor oil is very soothing and lubricating to the skin and hair because it is rich in fatty acids. It acts as a humectant, attracting moisture to the hair.

Almond

Description: Light weight with a slight, nutty fragrance.

Benefit: Enriched with vitamins and essential fatty acids, while combating dry skin and psoriasis.

Alma Oil

Description: Lightweight

Benefit: Healing vitamin C combined with natural properties reverses hair loss, and strengthen the hair at the root.

Shea Butter

Type: Unrefined

Description: Solid butter made from the fruit of the shea tree.

Benefit: Moisturizing and protective due to a unique fatty acid profile. Full of vitamins A & E, and natural antioxidants, which protect the hair from environmental stress.

Essential Oils*

Type: Tea Tree

Description: Earthy, spicy, warm aroma.

Benefit: Heals minor skin conditions, like dry scalp, and effective against psoriasis. The most effective anti-fungal, anti-viral and anti-bacterial essential oil.

Precautions: Tea tree can be used without dilution for spot treatment, however a patch test should be conducted 12 hours preceding complete treatment.

Type: Rosemary*

Description: Fresh, strong, clear aroma.

Benefit: Helps to heal scalp conditions, like dandruff, said to trigger hair growth.

Type: Peppermint*

Description: Very strong and piercing mint aroma.

Benefit: Stimulating and cooling to the scalp.

Type: Sage*

Description: Sweet, soft aroma with a hint of a musky/amber fragrance.

Benefit: Calming, adds freshness to thick hair and locs. Beneficial for solving scalp problems.

Type: Lavender*

Description: Earthy, spicy, warm aroma.

Benefit: Floral, fresh and light with a woody undertone.

Precautions: Excellent for childrens products, but be careful to dilute.

*General Precaution: Do your research and check with your physician before using, particularly if you have a medical condition.

Do not use if you are pregnant, have high-blood pressure, epilepsy, or are on medication.

Herbs

Type: Nettle

Description: Flowering plant with leaves that are high in chlorophyll, vitamin E, A & C, and other nutrients.

Benefit: Effective in soothing an itchy scalp, resolves dandruff issues, and excellent to use in hair preparations of all sorts.

Type: Rose Bud (or rose hips)

Description: Derived from an herbaceous shrub, full of vitamin C.

Benefit: Also contains vitamins C, E, K, B and a host of healing properties that are perfect for a healthy scalp. Carries emollient properties.

Type: Chamomile

Description: Hardy, evergreen, fragrant herb.

Benefit: A natural antioxidant and antifungal, chamomile is used as a conditioning agent for the hair.

Type: Lavender

Description: Floral, fresh and light with woody undertone.

Benefit: Eliminates germs and rejuvenates the hair and scalp.

Type: Horsetail*

Description: A brush-like plant derived from ferns that existed prehistorically, and has nutrient rich, healing qualities.

Benefit: Enriched with silica, which restores connective tissues and strengthens the hair and skin.

Type: Marigold

Description: Also called Calendula, an orange and yellow flowering plant found in North America and Europe.

Benefit: Soothing the scalp is the specialty of the marigold, and helps to heal the scalp with natural Vitamin C & E.

Type: Lemongrass

Description: A perennial fragrant herb.

Benefit: Known for its antibacterial and antifungal qualities, lemongrass helps to kill germs and to balance the skin.

*General Precaution: Do your research and check with your physician before using, particularly if you have a medical condition.

Do not use if you are pregnant, have high-blood pressure, epilepsy, or are on medication.

Other Essential Ingredients

Product: Filtered Apple Cider Vinegar (ACV)

Description: An acidic, sour liquid, resulting from the fermentation of apples.

Benefit: High acidity of malic acid and enzymes kill bottle bacillus, a bacteria that causes itchy scalp and dandruff, as well as thinning hair and baldness. The bacteria form scales and dry crust. ACV kills the bacteria and stimulates oil glands.

Product: Honey

Description: A substance made of a variety of sugars, beta-carotene, minerals, vitamins & enzymes.

Benefit: An all natural humectant, honey is one of the most naturally hydrating, pH balanced ingredients for moisturized hair.

Product: Aloe Vera Gel

Description: Vitamin and mineral rich Aloe Vera gel increases cell proliferation, promoting healing for the scalp.

Benefit: Aloe Vera Gel is soothing to the scalp and moisturizing to the hair. Look for food grade preservatives when possible.

Product: Lemon Juice

Description: Contains Vitamin C, A and Potassium, which promotes proper cell development.

Benefit: Helps to regulate the sebaceous glands, prevent dandruff and safely remove product build-up.

Product: Vegetable Glycerin

Description: Odorless, colorless, syrupy liquid that is a by-product of soap making.

Benefit: Like honey, vegetable glycerin is a natural humectant, and very moisturizing.

Product: Baking Soda

Description: Sodium bicarbonate, which is a soluble ionic salt.

Benefit: Soothes, cleans and deodorizes the hair and scalp, and is good for clarifying and restoring ph balance.

Product: Silk Peptide Powder

Description: A type of silk protein that is water soluble, and permeable, and contains 18 amino acids.

Benefit: As a source of protein, enhances elasticity and the spring of the hair, creates nutrient and moisture balance.

Product: Guar Gum

Description: A powder like substance derived from the guar plant.

Benefit: Thickens products without the use of heat. Use if you want to slightly solidify a liquid mixture for easier distribution throughout the hair.

Product: Rebatch Soap

Description: Basic natural soap.

Benefit: Can be purchased in blocks or shreds for easy use.

Where To Buy: Nappturous Diva Reveals her Organic Shopping Secrets!

It used to be that retail natural food stores were the only places that natural ingredients could be purchased, and then entered the internet!

Online shopping has created competition, which gives us, the buyers, an all-encompassing ability to comparison shop for the best deals! Let's not even mention what a little time and effort can produce on ebay.com, one of my favorite places to shop for natural ingredients for my homemade products.

Top stylists head to other online retailers, including www.anitagrant.com, for the best in vegan, organic ingredients, like whipped, unrefined shea butter and dried herbs.

Many options and the basics you need to start making your products can be attained in various kits assembled by Motown Girl and purchased from www.fromnaturewithlove.com. The popular NOW foods brand provides quality discount products that I have mentioned, including most of the carrier oils, essential oils, and supplements like wheatgrass. This brand can be found in local natural foods stores like Whole Foods, or by going to www.now-2-u.com.

Making your own product in bulk can positively impact your budget and help you to save more money! Do you love discounts? Join as a member at www.nappturality.com, and visit their forum topic Homemade Hair Products to get the discount codes for online shopping at some of the retailers I have listed here! Keep a look out for saving even more online and retail by joining preferred customer programs and scanning the clearance items for good finds.

For a complete menu of luscious natural products for your entire family, go to www.holisticbeauty.net!

Nappturous Diva's Favorite Fabulous Homemade Product Recipes

Some of my favorites are easy to make, as they combine one or two 100% nature based commercial products with handmade herbal infusions or unrefined shea butter, while others are just as simple to prepare, and are comprised completely of the best of the basic natural ingredients.

Either way, use these recipes as a springboard to selecting your own butters, essential oils and carrier oils for their therapeutic values, and combine them with other ingredients for a product that is your own handmade work of art!

Hair Recipes

Shampoo

Product: Baby Herbs Conditioning Poo

Ingredients: 3oz. Dr. Bronner's Baby Mild Shampoo, undiluted, and either 16oz. of Herbal Hair Tea (see recipe below), or 2 cups of distilled water, 5 drops each of peppermint, tea tree and lavender essential oils.

How to Prepare: Prepare 16oz. of Herbal Hair Tea or use 2 cups of distilled water and pour all ingredients into a bottle. Shake gently!

The herbs included in this gentle poo add sheen and body, and the Dr. Bronner's is a mild and effective cleaner. Use surplus as a body wash! Herb infusion must be used within 48 hours. For a longer lasting poo, use Option #2, which strengthens scalp health and promotes growth!

Pre-poo

Product: Hot Honey-Butter Condish

Ingredients: 8oz. of Shea butter, 4oz. of coconut oil, softened, 2 tablespoons of honey, 10 drops of essential oil of choice (optional)

How to Prepare: Soften the shea and coconut butters, measure and blend together with honey and essential oils. Apply to your hair while warm for a supremely lavish conditioner!

Product: Sweetness Condish

Ingredients: 4oz. Castor oil, 4oz. Amla oil, 2oz. honey, 4oz. lemon juice infused with 1 tablespoon of rosebud, chamomile, lavender and lemongrass herb mixture, 1 tsp. of Guar gum (do not include for locs)

How to Prepare: Warm the Castor oil, Alma oil and honey, and steep the herbs in warm lemon juice. Strain the lemon juice. Pour the oil and honey mixture, as well as the herb-infused lemon juice into a bowl. Mix and stir in Guar gum. Combine thoroughly. Section hair and apply from root to tip for hair that is moist, clarified, and never smelled so sweet! Rinse thoroughly.

Product: Silky Protein Mask (for the hair)

Ingredients: 4 oz. of Burt's Bees Avocado Pre-Shampoo Treatment or Avocado oil, 1 teaspoon Silk Peptide Powder, 2oz. Sweet Almond oil, 2oz. Aloe Vera Gel, 1oz. Vegetable Glycerin

How to Prepare: Combine Avocado with Sweet Almond oil and soften by warming. In a separate bowl, add the Silk Peptide Powder to the Aloe Vera gel, mixing well. Blend contents of both bowls together for a creamy, protein rich treatment that adds sheen and moisture. Apply to hair from root to tip. It's like a long, soothing drink of moisture to parched, dry hair! Leaves hair so soft!

Product: Whipped Coconut Cream Treatment

Ingredients: 4 oz. Coconut oil, 4oz. Olive oil, 2 oz. Shea Butter (Substitute Aloe Vera gel for locs), 10 drops of EO of choice, 5 drops Vanilla FO and 5 drops of Coconut FO.

How to Prepare: Soften ingredients, place in a bowl, add EO and whip with mixer until creamy. This easy recipe smells heavenly and treats hair with the gentle moisture it needs! Also can be used as a styling pomade!

Light Moisturizers

Product: BedHead Growth Spritz

Ingredients: 8 oz. distilled water, ½ oz. jojoba oil, 3 drops Sage EO, 5 drops of Peppermint EO, 5 drops Rosemary EO, Optional: 1oz. of Sisterlocks™ Moisture Treatment or other light conditioner.

How to Prepare: Mix ingredients in a spray bottle. Use to spritz "bedhead" away in the morning and to add an enriching yet fresh fragrance to your hair!

For even more moisture, add 1 oz. of melted Sisterlocks ™ Moisture treatment or other light conditioner, shake well and use daily! For added growth benefits, spray onto your scalp and give yourself a 5-minute invigorating scalp massage!

Styling Pomades

Product: Curly Frizz Vanilla Pudding

Ingredients: 9 oz conditioner (ND recommends **Karen's Body Beautiful Luscious Locks Moisturizing Hair Mask**), 3 oz Real Hair Gel (completely natural aloe hair gel), 1 oz vegetable glycerin, 1 oz Sweet Almond oil , 10 drops Rosemary EO (or EO of choice)

How to Prepare: Pour all ingredients into a bottle and shake well. Mixture should have a thick, but liquid viscosity.

Apply to wet tresses, and pull product through the hair, section by section. Seal with a light coating of jojoba oil. Allow to dry completely, and then pull the curls apart. Excellent for loose sets, twist sets, locs and styles on children and men!

Leave In Conditioner/Setting Lotion

Product: Moisture Gloss

Ingredients: 6 oz. Real Hair Gel (completely natural aloe hair gel), 2 oz. Jojoba Oil, 5 drops EO of choice

How to Prepare: Combine all ingredients in a bottle and shake well. The lightweight gloss adds moisture, body, and essential vitamins to hair and scalp, and is a great setting lotion and leave-in conditioner! For best distribution through hair, use a spray bottle to apply.

Clarifiers and Rinses

Product: Herb Infused Hair Tea

Ingredients: 2 cups distilled water, 1 tablespoon each of dried Horsetail and Nettle, 5 drops each rosemary, tea tree and peppermint oils

How to Prepare: Pour boiling water over the dried herbs, cover with saran wrap and allow to steep until cool. Pour into a clean spray bottle, add essential oils and shake well. Apply to hair and leave in or rinse. Use as a conditioning rinse as the base of your clarifying treatments and shampoos, or as a moisturizing water spritz. Seal any surplus in a jar and store in a cool place. Use within 48 hours.

Product: Refreshing Lavender & Baking Soda Clarifier

Ingredients: 2 cups distilled or Herb Infused Hair Tea, warmed, 1 tablespoon Baking Soda, 10 drops Lavender EO

How to Prepare: Warm the Herb Infused Hair tea and mix all ingredients in a spray bottle, shake thoroughly. Spritz your scalp, section by section, using the entire bottle. Use your fingers to massage the scalp for 2-3 minutes before rinsing. Also use as a no-poo option!

Product: Sweetness Hair & Scalp Treatment (clarifier)

Ingredients: 2 cups Herb Infused Hair Tea, warmed, 1 teaspoon honey, ½ cup ACV, 10 drops Essential oil of choice

How to Prepare: Prepare 2 cups of Herb Infused Hair tea, warm in microwave. Stir in 1 teaspoon of honey, ½ cup of ACV and essential oils. Apply to hair and scalp. No need to rinse. Seal any surplus in a jar and store in a cool place. Use within 48 hours.

Nappturous Diva Breaks It Down: How to Mix your Products at Home...A Quick Tip!

If you do not have a double boiler for warming your solid ingredients, instead of putting your products in the microwave, place hard ingredients in a small bowl, and place the bowl in a saucepan of boiling hot water. Let it sit until it melts to the desired consistency. To create a "whipped" version of any product, add air into the concoction by blending well using an eggbeater or mixer.

homemade&commercialproducts
Putting It All Together!

As you experiment with what works well for you, I've customized some product combinations using both commercial and homemade products that produce outstanding results as your hair regimen! The components of each regimen were selected for the ingredients they contain that specifically address and rectify the area of concern. To easily simplify the combinations for those who desire less product usage, use the same conditioner for the pre-poo and deep condition, clarify once a month, and use one moisturizer.

Dry Scalp/Dandruff

The goal of this dandruff routine is to get to the symptom of the problem, address it, and then provide the sustenance for a healthy head of hair. This routine accomplishes that goal by utilizing

ACV, an ingredient that kills the bacteria that cause dandruff, and honey, a humectant that draws moisture to the hair. Additionally, the use of peppermint essential oils in the Dr. Bronner's shampoo and in the Sweetness clarifying treatment, combined with tea tree, condition the scalp. For best results, massage your scalp during each stage of the regime, especially the shampoo, conditioner and clarifying treatment, for at least 5 minutes each.

Regime:

Pre-Poo: Hot Honey-Butter Condish (homemade)

Shampoo: Dr. Bronner's Peppermint Castile Soap

Deep Condition: Karen's Body Beautiful Luscious Locks Moisturizing Hair Mask

Clarify: Sweetness Hair & Scalp Treatment (use 5 drops of peppermint and 5 drops of tea tree essential oils) (homemade)

Moisturize: Alaffia Shea and Virgin Coconut Enriching Hair Lotion followed by Curls Pure Pomegranate Seed Oil Blend

Moisture Complex

Many of us consider ourselves experts on hair oil, but did you know that it takes more than just hair oil to help your hair maintain a smooth, supple reality? Conditioning is simple, and once you're armed with the tools for moisture, internally and externally, you'll reach your goal! Internally, ensure that your diet is healthy and you are drinking the appropriate amount of water daily. Externally, refrain from products with a chemical make-up, such as the majority of products you'll find in your local BSS, as the vast majority of their ingredients have a long-term drying effect on the hair. For a refresher, review **Nappturous Diva's Top Ingredients to Avoid.** Simplicity loves the basics, so go with what you know…and can pronounce!

Regime:

Pre-Poo: Whipped Coconut Cream Treatment (homemade)

Shampoo: Blended Beauty Soy Cream Shampoo

Deep Condition: Organikah Shea Butter Conditioner

Clarify: Sweetness Hair & Scalp Treatment (homemade)

Moisturize: Anita Grant Creamy Café Latte followed by Oyin Handmade Greg Juice

Growth Regimen

Watching your hair grow due to informed at-home care is rewarding, productive and fun! Besides your commitment to protective styling, you'll need products that naturally include growth ingredients directly from Mother Earth herself. These ingredients range from rosemary and sage, which stimulate growth, to avocado, a protein lover's choice! Moisture is enhanced by Aloe Vera and rich oils that leave your hair satisfied and soft.

Regime:

Pre-Poo: Silky Protein Mask (homemade)

Shampoo: Organikah, Herbal Shampoo

Deep Condition: Anita Grant Rhassoul Deep Condish

Clarify: Refreshing Lavender & Baking Soda Clarifier (homemade)

Moisturize: Curly Frizz Vanilla Pudding followed by Moisture Gloss (both homemade)

Locs

With locs, the key is to moisturize without over-conditioning, which can cause unnecessary slippage. This doesn't mean that you have to endure dry locs or scalp! Special attention needs to be taken to avoid product build-up; so light oils and humectants are included in this regime to increase the total moisture content in the locs. Shea butter and other thick, creamy ingredients are avoided, because once these ingredients build-up in the loc, they are difficult to remove and the wearer will find that their curls and styles will not hold as well due to product filled locs. The deep conditioning step is optional for locs, but if desired, a thinner, oil and herb based conditioner is preferable. The clarifying properties in the Sweetness Hair & Scalp Treatment leave a beautiful sheen on the locs, which are then ready for the ultimate moisture sealant, KBB's Hair Milk and a refreshing spritz of Zum Mist. Note: Skip the Deep Condition step if your locs are not yet mature.

Regime:

Pre-Poo: Sweetness Condish (homemade)

Shampoo: Baby Herbs Conditioning Poo (homemade)

Clarify: Sweetness Hair & Scalp Treatment (use 5 drops of sage and 5 drops of rosemary essential oils) (homemade)

Moisturize: Karen's Body Beautiful Hair Milk followed by Zum Mist

If you find that your hair is getting used to a regime, rotate through the above recommendations regularly with the seasons, or as your hair and scalp need! You can't go wrong when you do what feels right for your own hair.

Nappturous Diva's Principle #4

We Are Fabulous!

Translated, we are confident! If we have it, we work it. We never let an ill-informed person, whether that be a relative, stylist or bystander dictate how we feel about our hair. We choose to feel great about how we wear every single strand!

Principle #4 is last because the foundation has been laid for you to be inspired, educated and now, empowered to feel great about your hair choice and wear your natural hair proudly! The confidence that knowing why you are doing what you are doing combined with the ability to wear your hair in a manner that makes you happy create an irresistible nappturousity!

There are so many fabulous ways to wear healthy, natural hair. The main skill that you will need as you discover these methods and adapt them to your use is patience. It will take time to reach the ultimate goal you probably have in mind as you flip through magazines, and you will be encouraged to make the necessary investment of time as you view pictures of people who have tried to take a short cut and experienced short-term results. For long-term results that you can be proud of, I encourage you to enjoy the journey! Each stage of a natural transition can be found to be beautiful and enjoyable, if you know and experiment with what your hair will like!

When I transitioned to Sisterlocks™, I traded a huge, 10 inch afro for 4 inch, thin locs, and in the beginning, I almost wondered if that was the right decision! As soon as I could, I got a mirror and went to work on my hair. I discovered that the Basket-Weave updo was not only beautiful, but very functional, as it swept up the smaller locs and disguised the scalp that was showing in my newly loc'd hair. This style became my signature "fall-back" updo, and it did an excellent job as a semi-protective style, protecting the majority of the ends of my hair, and contributing to the current length and healthy condition of my locs.

In Principle #4, you will develop your own signature style plan, and complete the process of becoming a Nappturous Diva!

19

protective,semi-protective,**loose**&**rollover**styling

How do you feel about how you wear your hair, and which styles will look fabulous on you? What condition your hair is in, along with your hair goals, should be considered to answer these questions. If you are transitioning from a relaxer to natural hair, your primary choice of hairstyles may differ from the choice of someone who has been natural for a while and is pleased with their hair's current length and condition. The groups of styles that are displayed in this section include:

Protective styles: These are styles that help you to optimize the length and health of your hair by keeping the ends of the hair, which are the oldest and most prone to breakage, moisturized and tucked in. These styles require the least amount of manipulation and are excellent to wear year round, especially in the summertime! 100% of the ends of the hair are tucked away with Protective styling.

Semi-protective styles: This category includes styles that protect at least 50% of the hair.

Examples are styles that are swept back into a partial bun or up-do that allow some of the ends to be released towards the front. These styles are also good for transitioning and protecting the hair.

Loose styles: Loose styles require the most manipulation to wear, and are a fabulous option for showing off the body, length and condition of your hair. Because of the manipulation, these styles should be interchanged with Protective and Semi-protective styling options. Loose styles range from low-maintenance, as in the wash and go fro, to higher-maintenance, including twist-outs and braid-outs.

Rollover Styling

Have you been wearing the same hairstyle since you went natural? When you walk past a mirror, do you feel an overwhelming pressure to back up and do a double take at your fabulous, healthy hair? Are you satisfied with the nature of your styling abilities? If not, we are going to combat that problem right now, as this can be largely prohibitive. Rollover Styling is a term that I created to describe a cycle of different styles that you can wear with ease. Why change your style? Because wearing the same style all the time creates stress points, either around your hairline or within the hair. Changing your style allows you to protect your hair at times, and wear healthy hair loose when you choose.

Rollover styling takes one style and modifies it slowly, building off of the previous arrangement to create a different look. To know how long you should wear one of the styles in your Rollover styling routine, use the following formula:

Protective style, 60% + Semi-protective style, 30% + Loose style, 10% = Rollover styling!

Modifications to this formula can be made if your hair is less than 2 inches long and too short to arrange in a protective style. You may have to wear loose styles for a little while, but even the shortest hair can be braided back or twisted up and arranged by a professional.

If you are transitioning from a relaxer and have yet to cut the relaxed ends off of your hair, I advise you to wear your hair in Protective styles 90-100% of the time. The point on your hair where the natural and relaxed hair meet is a serious potential breaking point, and the less you are combing and manipulating your hair, the less breakage that will lead to split ends on your natural hair.

20
conclusion&stylegallery

Each of us has a certain flair, a sense of style and being that is showcased by wearing our hair naturally! With our crowning nappturosity, we can create a plethora of styles that give us options that fit our lifestyles, enjoy freedom and pass on a healthy self-esteem to the next generation. We also reach and exceed our goals for the development of our beauty, self-love and appreciation for what we have been given. As we near the end of this journey, we realize that the there really is no end, simply an ongoing development of peace and acceptance within. Thank you for taking this journey with me. Congratulations and welcome to Nappturous Diva-hood!

Style Gallery

Sisterlocks

Situation: The model wanted a style that would last at least three weeks and showcase the volume of her Sisterlocks.

Style Creation: This model's Sisterlocks were set using a bantu-knot set. Essentially, three or four locs at a time were spritzed with water and then twisted, section by section, in a clockwise mothion. The twist begins to curl down upon itself, and is twisted around into a circular "knot". The ends are tucked under the base of the "knot" to secure each bantu knot. The hair was allowed to dry. The bantu knots were released after the hair was completely dry, about three hours. The sections were separated to create a full, voluminous styles. This style will last 7-10 days.

Roll-over: We then created a roll-over style by separating the back of the hair into four sections, and flat twisting the sections from the nape of the neck up to the top of the head, and securing with a hairpin. Ths style will last for at least two weeks.

Natural Hair

Situation: The model was transitioning from relaxed to natural hair, and wanted a style that would disguise the two textures.

Style Creation: Using the Curly Frizz Vanilla Pudding (homemade), the models' hair was two-strand twisted. Due to the fine texture, the twists were then individually set on rod-style curlers. The models' hair was allowed to dry and all curlers were removed, then the twists were separated and fluffed.

Locs

The following pictures are provided by Mandisa Ngozi Braiding Gallery, photo credit: Keston Duke, New York, NY

Situation: The model wanted to add texture to her locs

Style Creation: Loc maintenance was conducted, and the models' locs were two-strand twisted while slightly damp. The locs were twisted in sections, allowed to dry, and then separated. The crinkled texture will last approximately two weeks.

conclusion

Each of us has a certain flair, a sense of style and being that is showcased by wearing our hair naturally! With our crowning nappturosity, we can create a plethora of styles that give us options that fit our lifestyles, enjoy freedom and pass on a healthy self-esteem to the next generation. We also reach and exceed our goals for the development of our beauty, self-love and appreciation for what we have been given. As we near the end of this journey, we realize that the there really is no end, simply an ongoing development of peace and acceptance within. Thank you for taking this journey with me. Congratulations and welcome to Nappturous Diva-hood!

For more information, or to connect with Erin, check us out on the following sites:

Our Home Site: www.naturalhairbook.com

Erin's Twitter Page: www.twitter.com/erinsanthony (@erinsanthony)

"Like" Nappturosity's Facebook Page: www.facebook.com/Nappturosity

Made in the USA
Lexington, KY
17 October 2012